T0329036

CAMBRIDGE LIBRARY COLLECTION

Books of enduring scholarly value

Education

This series focuses on educational theory and practice, particularly in the context of eighteenth- and nineteenth-century Europe and its colonies, and America. During this period, the questions of who should be educated, to what age, to what standard and using what curriculum, were widely debated. The reform of schools and universities, the drive towards improving women's education, and the movement for free (or at least low-cost) schools for the poor were all major concerns both for governments and for society at large. The books selected for reissue in this series discuss key issues of their time, including the 'appropriate' levels of instruction for the children of the working classes, the emergence of adult education movements, and proposals for the higher education of women. They also cover topics that still resonate today, such as the nature of education, the role of universities in the diffusion of knowledge, and the involvement of religious groups in establishing and running schools.

Practical Hints to Young Females

Displaying her intellectual and literary abilities from a young age, 'Mrs Taylor of Ongar' (1757–1830) enjoyed writing all her life. She had eleven children, of whom six (four of them writers) survived to adulthood. Her published works began with advice books for her own daughters, produced when increasing deafness made ordinary conversation difficult for her. Given the difficulty of providing advice equally appropriate to girls at all levels of society, this 1815 work is addressed to 'females in the middle ranks'. It is assumed that a girl's aspiration, as well as her destiny, is to be a wife and mother: conduct towards the husband, and the rearing of children, are of prime importance. But there is also a chapter for the husband, pointing out his reciprocal duties to his wife as an equal partner in their relationship. The book offers fascinating insights into the middle-class ideal of domestic happiness.

Cambridge University Press has long been a pioneer in the reissuing of out-of-print titles from its own backlist, producing digital reprints of books that are still sought after by scholars and students but could not be reprinted economically using traditional technology. The Cambridge Library Collection extends this activity to a wider range of books which are still of importance to researchers and professionals, either for the source material they contain, or as landmarks in the history of their academic discipline.

Drawing from the world-renowned collections in the Cambridge University Library and other partner libraries, and guided by the advice of experts in each subject area, Cambridge University Press is using state-of-the-art scanning machines in its own Printing House to capture the content of each book selected for inclusion. The files are processed to give a consistently clear, crisp image, and the books finished to the high quality standard for which the Press is recognised around the world. The latest print-on-demand technology ensures that the books will remain available indefinitely, and that orders for single or multiple copies can quickly be supplied.

The Cambridge Library Collection brings back to life books of enduring scholarly value (including out-of-copyright works originally issued by other publishers) across a wide range of disciplines in the humanities and social sciences and in science and technology.

Practical Hints
to Young Females

*On the Duties of a Wife, a Mother,
and a Mistress of a Family*

ANN TAYLOR

CAMBRIDGE
UNIVERSITY PRESS

CAMBRIDGE
UNIVERSITY PRESS

University Printing House, Cambridge, CB2 8BS, United Kingdom

Cambridge University Press is part of the University of Cambridge.

It furthers the University's mission by disseminating knowledge in the pursuit of
education, learning and research at the highest international levels of excellence.

www.cambridge.org
Information on this title: www.cambridge.org/9781108076241

© in this compilation Cambridge University Press 2015

This edition first published 1815
This digitally printed version 2015

ISBN 978-1-108-07624-1 Paperback

This book reproduces the text of the original edition. The content and language reflect
the beliefs, practices and terminology of their time, and have not been updated.

Cambridge University Press wishes to make clear that the book, unless originally published
by Cambridge, is not being republished by, in association or collaboration with,
or with the endorsement or approval of, the original publisher or its successors in title.

FRONTISPIECE.

Published Dec. 6, 1814, by Taylor & Hessey, 93, Fleet Street.

PRACTICAL HINTS

TO

𝔜oung 𝔉emales,

ON

THE DUTIES OF A WIFE,

A

MOTHER,

AND A

MISTRESS OF A FAMILY.

BY MRS. TAYLOR,

𝔒f 𝔒ngar,

AUTHOR OF ' MATERNAL SOLICITUDE FOR A
DAUGHTER'S BEST INTERESTS.'

' Every wise woman buildeth her house, but the foolish
plucketh it down with her hands.'—SOLOMON.

SECOND EDITION.

LONDON:

PRINTED FOR TAYLOR & HESSEY, 93, FLEET STREET,
AND J. CONDER, ST. PAUL'S CHURCHYARD.

1815.

J. MOYES, PRINTER,
Greville Street, Hatton Garden, London.

ADVERTISEMENT.

It is not easy to form rules, or even to suggest principles of practice, in such a manner as shall render them applicable to individuals of every class; and it will be obvious, upon a perusal of this little Work, that no attempt of the kind has here been made. Females in the middle ranks of society, in those especially which include numerous occupations and confined circumstances, are more immediately addressed; and to them many of the following observations assume to be of essential importance: but, at the same time, a hope is indulged, that readers of a different description may gain an occasional hint, by which their conduct in domestic life may be improved.

The parties more expressly in view are exempt (perhaps happily,) from that notoriety and distinction by which the family arrangements of such as move in the upper walks of life are too frequently disturbed : yet they occupy a station of sufficient eminence to render their conduct highly important to society. If it does not necessarily expose them to dissipation, much less does it degrade them into vulgarity or insignificance, as the degree of intellectual cultivation to be found among them evinces; for it is not every citizen in our days who is a *John Gilpin;* nor is every farmer a rustic. And although the influence of

good example in the middle ranks can
be but small upon those which are more
elevated; yet it descends like a kindly
shower upon such as are beneath them,
and gives fertility to many a spot which
would otherwise have remained sterile
and unsightly : so that, (to adopt the
expressive language of inspiration,) instead of the brier, comes up the myrtle;
and the wilderness blossoms as the rose.

By appropriate hints to increase the
respectability of this numerous class, is a
design, therefore, which immediately, or
remotely, affects so large a proportion of
the community, that it might discourage
the attempt of an humble individual.
But if to promote domestic virtue, and
preserve the happiness of the fireside, is

an effectual, as well as a simple means
of increasing national prosperity ; how
many are there, who have hitherto deemed themselves incompetent, whose efforts
might thus contribute to the public weal!

If this were not the case, and if effects
the most beneficial were not often produced by very humble means, the present
attempt had never been made by

THE AUTHOR.

CONTENTS.

	Page
INTRODUCTION	1
Conduct to the Husband	11
Domestic Economy	19
Servants	36
Education	45
Sickness	82
Visitors	91
Keeping at Home	106
Recreation	115
The Step-Mother	121
To the Husband	130
Conclusion	145

PRACTICAL HINTS,

&c.

No. I.

INTRODUCTION.

THERE was a time when females of rank and affluence were not thought degraded by dressing the fatted calf, and baking cakes upon the hearth; when, with their pitcher on their shoulder, they went to the well to draw water for their flocks; and when even royalty knew how to appreciate the virtues of her who sought wool and flax, and wrought willingly with her hands; who laid her hands to the spindle and to the distaff; who made fine linen and sold

B

it, and delivered girdles to the merchant;
who looked well to the ways of her household,
and ate not the bread of idleness. But time
has wrought a change in the circumstances
and habits of females of the present age,
though there are many of all ranks who are
not less usefully employed than were the
matrons of ancient times; many to whom it
may be said, ' Give them of the fruit of their
doings, and let their own works praise them
in the gate.' Happy the female in whom education has united with natural talent to form
so important a character as that of the *mistress
of a family;* and unhappy she, who, possessing
neither of these advantages, has the temerity
to undertake a task to which she is altogether
incompetent. Notwithstanding that *old wives,*
or *young wives,* may furnish the witling with
themes for ridicule, a closer observation would
convince him, that the *mistress* and *mother* of
a family occupies one of the most important
stations in the community; of which he would
be feelingly convinced, were so large a portion
of it to suspend its services for ever so short a
period.

We are, however, obliged to acknowledge, that the deficiencies of many have afforded but too just occasion for the sarcasms to which we allude. Nothing less than a more judicious education can remedy this vital evil; an evil which pervades all classes in some degree, but which is peculiarly injurious to those of the middle ranks. Many a female, because she has been educated at a boarding-school, returns home, not to assist her mother, but to support her pretensions to gentility by idleness, dress, and dissipation. She conceives herself degraded by domestic occupation, and expects to lose her credit if she is known to be industrious; while the fond parents too frequently aid the delusion, and in due time transfer her to a husband, to *curse* him with a fortune of a few hundreds; a sum which she supposes inexhaustible; accordingly she takes care to remind him, on every occasion, of the handsome fortune she brought him, as well as of the gentility of her *boarding-school* education. With what pity do we anticipate the sequel; and how many, who might have been formed to inestimable characters, have been

B 2

thus rendered worse than useless to society!
To afford a hint to such, as well as to those
who, from various other causes, may be incompetent to the duties of this important station, is the object of the following pages: and
it is hoped that some of the observations introduced may be found suitable to their circumstances, and deserving their attention.

Many, when they enter the married life,
assume a consequence to which their characters by no means entitle them. To be a wife,
and to be a *good wife*, which is from the Lord,
are two very distinct things: and if you, my
dear reader, have no just claim to the latter
title, that of the former will soon dwindle into
insignificance. The situation in which you are
placed is of vast, of vital importance; support
the dignity of it by your conduct, and add not
to the number by which it is brought into
disrepute and contempt. The mothers of
those who have decided the fate of empires
were once young wives, such as you are; and,
perhaps, the happiness or misery of thousands
then unborn originated in their conduct. But,

should the influence of your posterity never extend beyond the limits of private life, the effects of your conduct will yet be sufficiently important to warrant an earnest expostulation. Indeed your own respectability and happiness so immediately depend upon those of your family, that in neglecting the latter, the former are unavoidably undermined. Some there are who contrive to plod through life, without any failings prominent enough to incur the censure of their acquaintance, and pass in the crowd for mighty good sort of women: though it does not invariably happen that their families possess even these negative advantages: such have probably sunk into insipidity of character, from want of a timely stimulus and proper direction; and talents, which either lie dormant, or are wasted in trivial pursuits, might have been rendered, by early assistance, extensively useful. Many others, who, from their conduct in life, but too justly incur the censures of society, might equally with these have merited its applause, had some friendly hand been stretched out at the commencement of their journey, to guide them in the difficult and dubious way. To ensure so happy a result, let it be your ambition, my dear reader, to form a sterling character; and, while you contemplate women who command your esteem, endeavour to become estimable yourself: while others act desultorily, without design, and from mere impulse, do you proceed on principle; or, while their aim is fashion, let yours be steadiness.

There are two extremes into which young people are apt to fall, perhaps equally inimical to respectability of conduct: the one is *confidence*, the other *timidity*. The former, without doubt, is the most decided enemy to improvement; it renders the character ridiculous, and deprives it of a thousand advantages, by which the humble and teachable are benefited : but, where the latter predominates, the result is nearly the same; want of courage is mistaken for inability ; and, from fear of making an effort, no effort is made.

Where, however, as in the majority of instances, there is no material deficiency in the

intellectual powers, much may be effected by
well-timed advice, encouragement, or admo-
nition; and those whose age and experience
qualify them for the service, ought conscientiously to avail themselves of proper occasions upon which to render it.—Some years
ago, a lady, who went with a party to the
British Museum, expressed contempt and dis-
satisfaction at every thing she saw; protested
it was loss of time to continue, and urged the
company to hasten their departure. At length
they politely thanked the gentleman in attendance, and were about to withdraw, when he
detained them by the following address to
their fastidious companion: ' When I first saw
you, madam, I was struck with your beauty
and interesting appearance; but you soon gave
me occasion to alter my opinion: I pity the
man that marries you, if any one ever will;
certainly I would not; and I fear for you,
unless some alteration takes place in your
taste, manners, and habits.—Madam, I wish
you a good morning.' Many years after, the
same gentleman waited upon another com-

pany at the Museum: when they took their
leave, and thanked him for his polite attentions, a lady stepped forward, and expressed
her gratitude in a manner more lively than the
occasion seemed to require. The gentleman,
rather surprised, professed himself happy in
having contributed to her amusement. ' Sir,'
said she, ' my obligations to you far exceed
those which you have conferred this morning.'
She then recalled to his memory the above
circumstance; and added, ' I am that lady;
and to you I am indebted, next to this gentleman, who is my husband, for the happiest
influence on my life and character; arising
from the very pointed, but salutary, reproof
which you then administered.'

It is no wonder if the traveller, who is
unacquainted with the road, should sometimes
turn wrong, or be so entangled in intricate
windings as to be unable to retrace his steps;
nor is it too great a stretch of candour to
believe, that many of the actions, which afford
copious matter for the tongue of calumny, or

just ground for reproof, are the result not so much of ill-intention, as of inconsideration or mistake. But mistakes, which may involve families in ruin, or render them miserable, it becomes of the utmost importance to rectify; especially if we take into the account the influence which they have ultimately on the general weal. One of the most prominent, and fatal in its consequences, is the propensity to assume, by external appearance, a rank in society to which the finances are inadequate. This, indeed, is a conduct which rarely succeeds; for, till one rank can assume the manners and habits of those above them, it is in vain that they ape their dress and equipage; they will generally remain stationary in the eyes of all who know them, and even of all who do not; as the servant girl, who, taking the pattern of her mistress's cap, remains a servant girl still, and exposes herself to ridicule for her presumption. As nothing is more common than this destructive ambition, though so little is really gained by it, some of

the subsequent pages shall be devoted to
the consideration of this, and the opposite
line of conduct: but previously we shall
treat of more important matters.

No. II.

CONDUCT TO THE HUSBAND.

THE first object that should claim your attention, is that being with whom you have united your fortunes. When he vowed to take you for better for worse, he staked the happiness of his future life; a treasure for which the most ample portion is insufficient to compensate. On your part, you promised to *love* as well as to honour and obey; and probably from the all perfect being to whom you then surrendered yourself, you expected to derive such uninterrupted felicity as would render the fulfilment of this promise constantly easy and delightful. But, however discreet your choice has been, time and circumstances alone can sufficiently develop your husband's character: by degrees the discovery will be made that you have married a mortal, and that the object of your affections is not entirely free from the infirmities of human nature. Then it

is, that by an impartial survey of your own character, your disappointment may be moderated;
and your love, so far from declining, may acquire
additional tenderness, from the consciousness
that there is room for mutual forbearance.

Should your husband's temper be of the
placid and gentle kind, endeavour to perpetuate
it, even though your own may not naturally be
of that description, and you will have a
powerful incentive to imitation in observing
the benign effects of such dispositions on
yourself and others: especially recollect, that
nothing is more contagious than bad temper,
and that a disordered mind, as well as a diseased body, may spread infection over a whole
house. — Should he be morose, fretful, or
capricious, liable to sudden sallies, or the prey
of constant irritability, the cure cannot be
effected by opposing similar qualities; by these
the evil would be increased and perpetuated:
but their contraries, sweetness, the coolness of
a reasonable mind, and that kindness which
anticipates the causes of irritation, or allays
and sooths it when it is excited, even if they

failed to produce the change in his feelings
that might be expected, would at least have
the most salutary influence upon your own,
and bring a revenue of peace to the mind
under all its trials. There is one simple direction, which, if carefully regarded, might
long preserve the tranquillity of the married
life, and insure no inconsiderable portion of
connubial happiness: it is, to *beware of the*
FIRST *dispute.*

As the head of a family, you must expect to
meet with provocation, and to find your
patience continually called to the proof; but
you are utterly unfit to command others if you
cannot command yourself; and that is a lesson
which ought to have been previously learned,
for it will be difficult to acquire when pressed
by business and surrounded by vexations,
which demand its immediate and perfect
exercise. Destitute of a qualification so important, you cannot acquit yourself well; and
possessing it, you will probably rule even over
your husband with a sway which he will not
be inclined to dispute, and of which you need

not yourself be ashamed. There cannot, indeed,
be a sight more uncouth, than that of a man
and his wife struggling for power; for where
it ought to be vested, nature, reason, and
scripture, concur to declare : but the influence
acquired by amiable conduct and self-command does not fall under this censure. She
whose predominant passion is the love of sway,
has certainly mistaken her object when she
exercises it upon her husband. How prepos-
terous is it to hear a woman say, ' It *shall*
be done!'—' I *will* have it so!' and often
extending her authority not only beyond her
jurisdiction, but in matters where he alone is
competent to act, or even to judge. A man
of common understanding, though he may
derive benefit from his wife's advice, certainly
ought not to be governed by her : and as the
fool saith to every one ' I am a fool,' it is
presumed that whoever has the misfortune to
be united to such a one, might have previously
made the discovery, and can only have herself
to blame. But the woman who can tyrannize
over her husband, will generally betray the
same disposition towards her children, her

servants, and her acquaintance. By all of
these she may contrive to be feared; and, as
it is probable that to be loved is no part of her
ambition, she escapes the mortification of
disappointment: but, my young friend, I would
hope better things of you, and that to deserve
and ensure the affections of your family is the
virtuous satisfaction at which you continually
aim.

In order to cherish these kindly feelings,
accustom yourself, in the contemplation of
your husband's character, to dwell on the bright
side; let his virtues occupy your thoughts
more than his failings: this will impel you to
honour him in the presence of others, and may
eventually produce the happiest effects on his
character; for most probably he will feel the
value of that estimation in which you hold
him, and be solicitous to preserve it.—Do not
expose his failings; no, not to your most
confidential friend. If, unhappily, they are of
the more flagrant kind, he divulges them
himself; but if, on the contrary, they are merely
such as prove him to be a fallible creature,

leave your friends to infer it for themselves,
rather than furnish them with proofs of it
from your complaints. Your own failings
(should you have any) you would studiously
conceal; and probably you think it the duty of
your husband to conceal them too: but the
golden rule of doing to others as you would
they should do unto you, does not apply, in
this case, with sufficient force; because it is
your very self, your better self, who would suffer
by such an exposure; his honour and yours
are inseparably one.

It has been observed, that you have united
your fortunes: how absurd then would it
be to urge your husband to expenses beyond
his income! how thoughtless, to forget that
you must stand or fall together!—There are
many, who, instead of restraining those gene-
rous spirits that would make costly sacrifices
to love, have adopted the ruinous system of
getting all they can; not considering that they
are but taking out of one pocket to put into
another, or foreseeing the consequence, in
having both pockets empty. But young

women, who have been profusely supplied with
money by their parents, are often not sufficiently aware of its value : those who, while
single, have been accustomed only to ask and
have, to have and spend, will rarely make
careful or economical wives; and hence ap-
pears the utility of parents allowing their
daughters a stipulated, but moderate sum, for
their dress and other expenses at an early age :
this will inure them to habits of economy, and
restrain them from being lavish in domestic
expenditure. Hence too the benefit of admit-
ting them to family confidence, and making
them acquainted with the general state of
affairs. In most cases, they will thus discover
that income, however abundant, is not quite
inexhaustible, and that there may be such a
thing as living beyond it. Of this simple truth
it is especially important that a wife should be
convinced, though to the minds of some it
seems never to have occurred.

There are few husbands so adroit in the
management of their incomes as to be entirely
able to defend them from dissipation, where

ignorance or extravagance are the character-
istics of the wife. Vain are his labours to
accumulate, if she cannot, or will not, expend
with discretion. Vain too are his expectations
of happiness, if economy, order, and regularity,
are not to be found at home: and the woman
who has not feeling and principle sufficient to
regulate her conduct in these concerns, will
rarely acquit herself respectably in the more
elevated parts of female duty. We shall
therefore request permission to introduce a
subject which, though less sentimental than
some we have already noticed, has often an
equal influence on the happiness of the married
life.

No. III.

DOMESTIC ECONOMY.

THE minute details into which we are about
to enter, in this chapter, may seem beneath
the dignity of instruction : but if general principles are thereby better understood, they will
not require apology. Even an astronomer,
reasoning upon the planetary system, resorts
to a diagram of a few simple lines, and explains clearly the most sublime or intricate
doctrines by this means. Without further
preface then, we shall place at the head of the
present subject, a simple calculation, which
forms a sage, but neglected maxim, ' *A penny
a day is thirty shillings a year.'*

Were this habitually kept in view, how
many superfluous expenses would be curtailed!
It would raise the character of that degraded
thing a *penny*, to its proper value ; pence
would accumulate till they became pounds ;

and, like a well-disciplined troop surrounding
our possessions, would prevent insidious depredation, and often keep poverty at bay. It is
to be feared, that few of those who frequently
say, ' It is *but* a penny,' will become possessed
of pounds by their own prudence and management. Yet a penny a day does not suffice such
persons as these to disregard and to squander;
the same disposition pervades their whole conduct, and is a constant drain upon their pecuniary resources: probably every article with
which they are concerned will pay its tribute
to the idol of extravagance ; and the amount
of such a daily tax it is fearful to calculate.
That this calculation may not eventually be
made by the creditor, an account book is
earnestly recommended; printed ones may be
had with columns for every article, and for
every day in the year : and to those who are
so frequently wondering which way their
money goes, this would have the effect of de-
monstration; it would do away all that was
mysterious in the business, and convince them
that they have neither had holes in their
pockets, nor been robbed. Many persons

satisfy themselves with keeping an account of
the larger sums they expend; but these can
generally be recollected; while the shillings
and sixpences pass away in great numbers, and
almost imperceptibly, because deemed too
trifling for notice. A strict account of these
would at a glance convince of their importance.
It would exhibit, at one view, the enormous
amount of money expended in gloves, ribands,
and other articles of haberdashery, in which
some young women are thoughtlessly profuse ;
and it might prove a more effectual antidote
to the passion for *great bargains*, than any
that could be written upon the subject. It is
certain, that though the affluent may occasionally indulge themselves in purchasing articles
they do not want, or perhaps never may,
those who are *not* affluent should by no means
allow such a propensity; lest while a *great
bargain* is lying by useless, they should actually be in want of a common necessary.
Some years ago, a female, who had by im-
prudence reduced herself to her last ninepence,
was prevailed upon, by its *cheapness*, to pur-
chase a pretty box for the reception of threads

and tapes! Alas! it was doubtful whether she
would ever more be mistress of either tapes
or threads!

If that money which is spent by the young
and inconsiderate, in a desultory or superfluous manner, were kept in reserve to supply
the place of each useful article, as it is laid
aside; it would be very advantageous to those
whose finances render it difficult to make
large purchases. To such it is of great importance to keep up the original stock; and if
they were, at stated times, to put by a certain
sum, however small, they would have a little
fund constantly rising, and be exempted from
those anxieties which many, for want of better
management, endure. Should this plan be
thought eligible, let servants' wages especially
be included; and if the day upon which they
became due were previously marked in the
account-book, it would ensure their punctual
payment, and the wages of the hireling would
not be kept back, either by lack of means or
treachery of memory. A poor girl, who
goes to service with a scanty wardrobe, has

often to endure inconveniences, or incur debts, through the negligence of her employers, which a little attention on their part, to her necessities and feelings, would easily prevent.

Much loss is sustained by purchasing articles of housekeeping in small quantities; not only as to their original cost, but in their consumption, as many of them are benefited by keeping : nor can regular weekly payments be too forcibly recommended. It is frequently impossible to ascertain whether a bill of even a month's standing is quite correct; and many who are tempted to let them run still longer, increase with the delay the probability of not paying them at all : those who are honestly determined that they shall be paid, would find it more prudent and less difficult to discharge them weekly, and thereby at once defend their own property, and ensure that of their tradesmen.—A housekeeper who had adopted the injudicious practice of paying but once a year, having *equally* divided his custom between two bakers, found that one of them had charged him for a quantity of bread just twice as

much as he had had from the other! Tradesmen are not all dishonest, but all are liable to
mistakes, many of which in a long account
cannot be rectified.

A discreet housekeeper will distinguish between necessary and unnecessary expenses : as
no one can work without tools, every house
ought to be furnished with appropriate uten-
sils, or there will be great confusion and inconvenience in domestic business. A deficiency of this kind is sometimes supplied by
borrowing of neighbours, and leaving them no
alternative between the injury of their goods
by continual use or removal, and a negative
which they would feel it painful to give. It is
astonishing to what inconveniences some people subject themselves and their unfortunate
neighbours for years, to save the expense of a
few shillings, perhaps a few pence ; forgetting
that while they are sending to next door, or
across the way, they may lose more time than
the borrowed article is worth. Yet the contrary extreme should be avoided, and whim
not mistaken for necessity : many *handy*

things may be dispensed with, and the money
they would cost, which, if properly employed,
is the handiest thing of all, devoted to more
useful purposes.

But if small inadvertent expenses may become serious in the aggregate, what must be
the result of a style of dress and appearance
throughout, to which the circumstances are
unequal ! Many persons are so adroit in
purchasing, in cutting and contriving, that
they can obtain articles at a much cheaper
rate than others: but perhaps when reduced
by those means to their lowest cost, the
amount not only exceeds what ought to
be afforded, but the article so obtained ill
accords with the rank in life, or confined
income, of the purchaser, and only exposes her
to ridicule or censure. Those who obtain for
four pounds that which is worth five, are
neither to be praised nor envied, if two were
as much as they ought to have spent.—A
smart young couple were once passing the
door of a tradesman to whom they owed a
small sum of rather too long standing, when

c

the creditor was heard to exclaim, ' See how
fine they are! they had better pay their
debts.' Now it happened that .their finery
had cost them nothing, for it was furnished
by their kind but ill-judging friends ; this,
however, the tradesman could not know, nor
do lookers on in general either know or
care, *how* finery is obtained; but they do
know whether situation and appearance cor-
respond, and they make their animadversions
accordingly.

Next to the knowledge of *what to get*, is
the necessary study of *how to keep*. It is
astonishing at what a small expense some
persons will maintain a genteel appearance :
and here I hope I shall not be thought *too*
minute, if I allude to the care which is requisite to apparel *off* as well as *on;* permit me
to say, that articles neatly dusted, brushed,
folded, and laid in a place of safety, will retain
their beauty for a length of time, of which
those who never made the experiment would
be incredulous. It is also to be wished, that
mothers, in those ranks where income is usu-

ally small, would initiate their daughters well
in the art of repairing; it is an indispensable
part of female economy, and its humble tro-
phies would be in reality more honourable,
as well as more useful, than the finest piece of
embroidery ever sent in from a boarding
school : much comfort, in families that are
not affluent especially, depends upon the
' stitch in time.'

That house only is well conducted, where
there is a strict attention paid to order and
regularity. To do every thing in its proper
time, to keep every thing in its right place,
and to use every thing for its proper use, is
the very essence of good management, and is
well expressed in one of the Lancasterian
establishments, ' the rule of this school is
to have a place for every thing, and every
thing in its place.' While some think they
have no time to put things away, others assert
that they have no time to misplace them; no
half hours to spare in searching for lost goods.
The time of every individual *ought* to be precious ; with the mistress of a family it is pe-

c 2

culiarly so; and a proper adjustment of this
cannot be too forcibly inculcated. Meals
should always be ready at the stated time; and
servants, if possible, obliged to be punctual :
but to effect this, and prevent confusion, they
must receive clear and early orders. Early
rising, where the health will permit, produces
more advantages than the mere lengthening
of the day. An honest labouring man said
once, very significantly, to a gentleman in
whose neighbourhood he lived, 'I observe, sir,
you are up very early of a morning: I believe, if all housekeepers would do the same,
they would find their account in it at the
year's end.' This has often been found to
be true, Where servants are ill disposed, and
their employers are known to be safe in their
chambers till a late hour, depredations to no inconsiderable amount may easily be carried on.

There are some who complain that the day
is too long; others, that it is too short: for
the former there is no excuse : and many of
the latter would find it difficult to produce one,
were they told of the desultory manner in

which they pass their time. Those who will
sit an hour idle over the fire at dusk light, to
save an inch of candle, must not complain of
being busy : it is probable that if others were
to value their time no more than they appear
to do themselves, they would resent the appa-
rent injustice.

The hints that have here been given, are mere
hints, and form a small proportion of those
which the subject of domestic economy sug-
gests : but some may think them already too
minute, and others may even object to the
principles upon which they are founded : if,
however, they would take the trouble to look
around them in the world, instances would
not be wanting to sanction and enforce both
the principles and the particulars. For the
accommodation of some readers, one shall
be selected from a number known to the
author.

A gay young person of nineteen, who had
married a respectable tradesman soon after
she left a boarding school, had a young friend

in similar circumstances, who was lamenting
their mutual ignorance, and expressing her
fears lest they should be unable, little as they
knew of domestic management, to acquit them-.
selves well in their new situations. ' Dear me !'
was the reply, ' I do not trouble my head
about that ; the maids will do those things.'
This, with the disordered state of her wardrobe, and many symptoms of a similar nature,
excited in her friend, who had rather more
thought, no very sanguine hopes of her success. It is almost superfluous to record the
sequel: her husband was a bankrupt in two
years! So well had the maids managed for
her !

There are honourable examples of an opposite class; but they are too rare; and should
any of my readers be disposed to imitate them,
they must pay the price, *and dare to be singular;* for if among their own acquaintance
they lack a precedent, they must venture to
make one. Should they wish to maintain their
rank in society, it will be better preserved by
having it said, that they have more than they

spend; than, that they spend more than they ought. It is true that he who will be rich at any rate pierceth himself through with many sorrows; but 'give me neither poverty nor riches,' is a petition not unbecoming a Christian. A decent competence, as it exempts from preying anxiety, and from the temptation to mean contrivances and low subterfuges, ennobles the character; and, by expanding the heart, promotes feelings of benevolence, and cherishes a variety of Christian virtues; which are blighted, and sometimes totally destroyed, by pecuniary difficulties.

Persons who live up to their income are totally unprepared for sudden contingencies: having neglected common forethought, they are little likely to extricate themselves from embarrassments, in which they may unexpectedly be involved; and are not unfrequently brought, therefore, into circumstances the most insupportable to a well-constituted mind; they become dependant upon, and burdensome to, others.

My young friend, if you have children, how
anxious are you that every want shall be
supplied! Perhaps you are one of those who
indulge all their caprices, and can deny them
nothing. You would be shocked to be compared with the brute species, who, after all
their indulgence, at length turn their young
adrift, nor cherish them more: yet your
conduct bears too near a resemblance to
theirs, if, from thoughtlessness or extravagance, you make no provision for them
against they attain your age, and are in your
circumstances. If you know the value of only
a few hundred pounds by the want of them,
one would think it would naturally suggest to
you the propriety of making some provision
for your children, however small it might be ;
and remember, that the fact of ' a penny a day
being thirty shillings a year,' if kept in view,
and applied prudently (not covetously) to your
domestic economy, will go a great way, in the
course of time, towards freeing them from
many of the anxieties, which at this moment
you may be enduring. ' He that provideth

not for his own house, is worse than an
infidel.'

But, whether you have children or not, the
period of old age will arrive to yourselves.
Some persons toil all their lives, and refuse
the enjoyments which can only be relished
when life is in its prime, that they may be rich
when the power of enjoyment is over. To
such, these pages are not addressed : but surely
it is desirable, after the heat and burden of the
day are over, to enjoy a degree of rest and
tranquillity, which narrow or embarrassed circumstances will not admit. How many at
this period are deprived, by their early im-
prudencies, of comforts to which they had
long been accustomed! How many too, from
the same cause, are compelled to turn a deaf
ear to the necessities of others, and thereby to
forego one of the highest gratifications of
which human nature is susceptible!

If reason should assent to any of these remarks, it will be wise to form corresponding
resolutions, and to act upon them with promp-

titude; for it is an awkward thing to make
great changes and adopt new habits, after
years of error and misconduct; though it is
better to improve late than never. Affliction
is the common lot of humanity; but there is
much that might be averted, and life rendered
not so dreary a season as some represent it, if
right views, and a right direction, were taken at
its commencement. It is an important truth,
and one that should be continually borne in
mind, that a large proportion of the evils
which overtake us, is fairly attributable to the
spirit of procrastination. We could scarcely
believe, did we not witness it every day, that
a traveller would knowingly take the wrong
road, for no other reason, perhaps, than because a few gaudy flowers grow on the way-
side; and often for no assignable reason whatever still proceed, though always intending to
turn back at some time or other. We could
scarcely believe, that what ought to be done
to-day should ever be carelessly postponed till
to-morrow, since to-morrow is laden with
duties of its own: trifles thus accumulated,
produce at length serious difficulties and em-

barrassments, from which the procrastinator, of all people, is the least qualified to extricate himself. If the incessant confusion in which such persons involve themselves and others, has become so habitual that they scarcely perceive the cause of the evil, let them discern their own character drawn to the life, and possibly something like their own fate predicted, in an admirable tale, entitled ' Tomorrow,' by Miss Edgeworth : it can scarcely fail to produce conviction ; and the next step to this is, or ought to be, amendment.

No. IV.

SERVANTS.

THAT servants have a considerable influence on the happiness of families, few, who have been long accustomed to the superintendance of them, will dispute. It is painful to hear the incessant complaints to which this subject gives rise, as they are strong indications of the continued depravity of the lower orders, notwithstanding the benevolent exertions of the last thirty years to banish ignorance, and vice as its offspring. This, indeed, no longer excites surprise, when it is considered how much the wholesome lessons dispensed at school, are counteracted at home. That such is the fact, those who are in the habit of visiting the cottages of the poor do not require to be informed: they meet, it is true, with some pleasing exceptions, but at present they are exceptions. We do not find upon every heath, or in every cottage, such characters as the

Shepherd of Salisbury Plain, nor in the daughters of every dairyman a *Dairyman's Daughter*. Parents who from ignorance are immoral, who have been unused either to observe or reflect, and whose habits are uncouth and vulgar, cannot be expected to render their children moral, observant, and considerate, or neat and skilful; nor ought the society to which most servants have been exposed, to be forgotten: a well-inclined girl is frequently ruined by her neighbours, or the companions of her servitude, who are much less likely, in general, to improve than to injure her. What wonder then, if, when we admit into our houses the children or associates of such, we find them without principle and without conduct, and apparently incapable of using either their eyes, their ears, or understandings! Why should we expect to gather grapes of thorns, or figs of thistles? To those who have passed their childhood in want and wretchedness, the sudden change which they experience when they enter service and are introduced to a plentiful supply, is another unfavourable circumstance; and is

not likely to make the thoughtless either frugal
or prudent: to plenty, they annex the idea of
riches, and suppose that any, and every thing,
can be afforded. A master can hardly appear
to them other than a being of a different
species, with whom they are totally unqualified
to sympathize, and in whose welfare they can
scarcely be expected to take much interest.

If therefore, from various causes, *good* servants are scarce, those who have large families,
and cannot conveniently keep more than one,
must not be disappointed if such do not fall to
their share. A *good* servant can always find a
good situation, among those who are both
able to appreciate her worth, and willing to
reward it : of course it is not likely that she
will take an inferior place; nor ought those
who have adopted the mistaken economy of
giving low wages, to expect much better
success. While some assert that they cannot
afford to give high wages, others shrewdly
maintain that they cannot afford to give low.
Persons who save three or four pounds a year
in this way, forget that nothing is gained in

board, and generally much more than an
equivalent lost by carelessness and want of
skill.

It cannot be doubted, that much of the evil
of which mistresses complain, would be reme-
died, if they would invariably adhere to giving
just and faithful characters. Every servant
should be told, when hired, that the *whole* of
her conduct will be communicated to her next
mistress: it is a false and ill judging lenity that
dictates an opposite conduct, and is eventually
injurious to both parties. Every one would
wish to receive a faithful character when she
applies for it herself, and should therefore be
conscientious in giving it, nor conceal even
little faults, of which there would be fewer if
this conduct were more generally adopted.
An author, who in a recent publication asserts,
that ' when you admit a servant into your
house, you admit an enemy,' perhaps ap-
proached too near the truth; yet he might
have expressed himself with less severity, had
he taken all the circumstances of the case
into consideration: at any rate, those who

would not wish to have their assent to his
opinion extorted by their own experience, will
be exceedingly cautious with regard to the
characters which they either take or give.

If housekeepers, where it is possible, would
put that work out which cannot be performed
at home without extra help, they would find
their account in it. Many a worthy girl has
been corrupted, and eventually ruined, by those
people who have access to families as chair-
women, &c.—they are too frequently depre-
dators in the houses which they frequent; and
it is well if in time they do not prevail upon
the servant to assist in their nefarious practices :
where they do nothing worse it is too frequently their custom to prejudice servants
against their places; and from these and similar objections, many judicious and expe-
rienced persons will on no account suffer them
to enter their houses.

But, notwithstanding all our endeavours to
obtain and to keep good servants, we shall
generally find much devolve upon ourselves:

and those certainly should not complain of
the remissness of their domestics, who are
themselves deficient in the art of management.
A little activity on the part of a mistress,
especially where but one servant is kept, will
give an agreeable finish to the appearance of a
house, and prevent many a reprimand for
inattention to the minutiæ; from which those,
at least, who have a redundancy of work, ought
to be exempted.

In every kitchen there should be a library,
for which a judicious selection of books will be
requisite, and nothing beyond the comprehen-
sion of kitchen readers admitted: but none in
the present day need be at a loss for appropriate works, when, beside other things, so
many excellent tracts may be procured for the
instruction of the poor. Perhaps Mrs. More's
Cheap Repository would stand pre-eminent in
such a collection; as the lessons there given,
and the examples exhibited, judiciously blend
amusement with instruction. And here let me
drop a hint respecting the choice of such
publications: many well-meaning and zealous

Christians really counteract the good they
intend to do, by refusing to distribute those
which are of a lively and entertaining nature,
forgetting that the readers they wish to serve,
require to be enticed to peruse, that they take
the alarm at an introduction too serious, and
rarely then go on to the end. Such persons
have been known to throw away tracts put
into their hands, merely from a sight of their
solemn and injudicious titles. Our Saviour
pursued a different course, frequently intro-
ducing parables of a very entertaining kind:
and were these zealous disciples to study
human nature in general, and especially the
heart in its unconverted state, they might
perceive the utility of those innocent baits,
which more judicious Christians may set to
catch souls. They appear not sufficiently to
distinguish between their own sensations, which
revolt at every thing that is not expressly
serious, and the sensations of those who revolt
still more against all that is.

But to return from this digression, let those
who are possessed of such a treasure as a *good*

servant, duly estimate their privilege, and be
neither too rigid in their requirements, nor too
sparing in their rewards. It is poor encouragement to a servant, if she is invariably
blamed for what is wrong, and never praised
for what is right; and some respect should be
paid to the feelings of human nature, which
will not endure continual chiding, however
deserving of it : both praises and rewards
should be suitably dispensed; and if, when
there is occasion to complain, appeals to reason
were more frequent than they generally are,
such reproof might have a gradual tendency to
improve the character. The old domestic
attached to a family, whose best days have
been spent in faithful services, is a lovely
character, and entitled to every indulgence :
and when an honest and tractable disposition
is observed in the young, self-interest alone
would dictate an endeavour to rear a servant
of this description, by care and kindness, by
mingling patience and forbearance with instruction or reproof. It is scarcely necessary
to add, that a good example must be set by
the mistress, in order to give effect to her

injunctions; for if her own character is tur-
bulent and disorderly, she has little reason to
anticipate regularity and comfort from her
domestics.

An additional hint to those young mistresses
who have not the knowledge requisite for their
situation, but who, conscious of their deficiency, wish to acquire it, shall close this
subject. A young and ignorant mistress will
rarely have a servant from whom she may not
gain, by *unobserved attention,* some useful
hints: from her last place something is generally brought that will turn to account; and
there are those who have obtained much of
their domestic knowledge from this source;
it is tedious and precarious, but if necessary
information can be obtained, those who are
destitute of it should not be too proud, or too
indolent, to avail themselves of every opportunity for acquiring it.

No. V.

EDUCATION.

In proportion as parents are sensible of the importance and difficulty of the work of education, will they be attentive to any offer of assistance, and solicitous to qualify their children for discharging similar duties, when it shall come to their turn to discipline and instruct. All admit that childhood is the time for instruction; but the term *discipline* sounds harsh in the ears of many a tender mother, because she has attached to it the idea of severity. No wonder, then, if even in this, the most important of all mortal concerns, she is tempted to procrastinate; no wonder if her resolution fails, when contemplating the lovely cherub with a mother's fondness; yet she would do well to consider, during those tender moments, that there may be other cherubs quite as interesting to their

parents, who may hereafter endure the acutest
sufferings, from their connexion with the darling whose passions she has not sufficient for-
titude to control; the darling, who must grow
a little older, and, of course, a little more
ungovernable, before the dreadful secret is re-
vealed to it, that all it sees, and all it wishes
for, is not its own!

It is a mistake, fraught with the most
disasterous consequences, to individuals, to
families, and eventually to communities, that
an *infant* is too young to be rebuked: not
long after it can distinguish the parent, and
know that from her it derives its nourishment, it may be made sensible of her displeasure, when evidently crying for passion:
but how inimical to its peace and happiness
are the absurd and mistaken notions respecting its crying, which are generally entertained!
People actually perpetuate what they wish
to prevent, by complying thus with every
caprice. The child who has learned that its
gratifications are not to be purchased by tears

and clamour, will soon forbear; will become
tranquil and peaceable, and afford reason to
hope, that so desirable a temper, improved by
a rational system of education, will accompany
it through life: while the being who has been
accustomed to have every wish gratified for
which it could cry, may one day have recourse to other means, more forcible than
crying, to obtain its object. Education, according to Mr. Howard, should commence
with the first dawn of the mental faculties;
and an anecdote is related by his biographer,
which exhibits a specimen of the discipline he
really adopted: ' His child one day wanting
something which he was not to have, fell
into a fit of crying, which the nurse could
not pacify. Mr. Howard took him from her,
and laid him quietly in his lap, till, fatigued
with crying, he became still. This process,
a few times repeated, had such an effect,
that the child, if crying ever so violently,
was rendered quiet the instant his father took
him. In a similar manner, without harsh
words and threats, still less blows, he gained
every other point which he thought necessary

to gain, and brought the child to a habit of
obedience*.'

The first process of education is easy and
simple, if not rendered otherwise by delay.
Should the reader happily be one of those
whose wayward passions were thus early
checked, she will bear her testimony to the
excellence of the principle. She has no
gloomy recollections attached to her infant
days: the gentle discipline she underwent was
at too early a period to leave any traces upon
her memory; the violence of self-will was soon,
but surely checked, and she has not sallied into
life with her hand against every one, and, of
course, every one's hand against her; as is the
case where passion has been suffered to domi-
neer without control.

It is a question, in some cases, whether
the *infants* of the rich or the poor are the

* When there is reason to fear that the child may
be injured by excess of crying, let it be pacified or
diverted by some other object; but by no means
that for which it first cried.

worst situated ? The former are frequently
exposed to a degree of neglect and suffering
in the nursery, which might damp the vivacity of some gay mothers, were they aware
of it: and those who are anxious to cultivate
amiable dispositions in their families, and to
preserve the simplicity and purity of their
minds, will intrust them as little as possible to
the care of servants and hirelings; rejoicing
if their rank in society, or small circle of what
are called friends, allows them the unremit-
ting superintendance of their bodies and minds.
The custom of not permitting children to sleep
with any but the most confidential domestics,
and not even with them any longer than is
absolutely necessary, cannot be too carefully
attended to : the evils of neglecting it are
great and various, as many have lamented,
and many more might confess. Servants, if
not ill-disposed, are, in general, too ignorant
to be trusted much alone with children: and
the terrors which a superstitious girl may
excite in their minds, are often so strong, as
to baffle the efforts of reason during many

D

succeeding years. Children have naturally,
or early acquire, a fear of ' the dark ; ' which
it is desirable as quickly as possible to remove ; but a few words dropt by a servant
relative to ' the ghost'—' the old man,'—or
some such mysterious personage, who is in-
voked, perhaps, to run away with the young
delinquent, may render every attempt to
dispel it for a long time unavailing. Another
practice, extremely injudicious, is that of
habituating a child to have some one, or
at least a light, in the room with it till it
falls asleep : this is to cherish fear, instead
of destroying it ; and when is it to be laid
aside ? When the poor child becomes old
enough to be beaten for wanting it ; and
when its imagination has acquired activity sufficient to increase and magnify the
images, which were too vague at first to have
made any deep impression upon its fears, if
judiciously repressed. A *father* has been
known to undress and go every evening to
bed with his *only* son, till he was ten or
eleven years of age. When the darling had

been by this means lulled to sleep, the parent was at liberty to creep down again to his friends or his business!

It is doubtful whether the bodies or the minds of children sustain the greatest injury from the inordinate gratification of their appetites. There are few adults, in our days, whose experience does not enjoin them to practise abstinence, sometimes in consequence of early indulgence; and, where this is the case, the habit of self-denial is very difficult to form, perhaps is never acquired; and a life of disease is endured for want of it. Others, whose constitutions have not suffered, have felt the baneful effects of a pampered appetite in distant periods of life; when, instead of having it gratified by what is *nice*, they have been deprived by poverty of common necessaries, and have then felt the contrast with double poignancy. Children should be accustomed to plain and wholesome food; should never, when in health, be permitted to choose for themselves, or to ask for this or that particular part or dish: nor will they do it,

but eat their meals peaceably, (a great help to
digestion,) if they find there is nothing to be
had but what is placed before them ; nothing,
especially, for asking or for crying for : they
should learn, as soon as possible, that man
does not live to eat; but that he eats to live.

How many family misfortunes are fairly
attributable to the love of dress ! How many
might be obviated if this destructive passion
were nipped in the bud ! if children were
early taught the original use of clothing, and
were mothers contented with keeping them
clean and warm ! There is so strong a propensity to decorate these objects of our affection, that an attempt to eradicate it is not
made with very sanguine hopes of success :
and such a copious source of maternal enjoyment might be left unmolested, were it not for
the injurious effects produced by it upon the
infant mind.   Yet, if there is a period when
the costume of a certain sect might prove
really advantageous, it is that of childhood ;
a period in which every bugle becomes the
prolific seed of vanity and extravagance.

What cost is frequently bestowed upon an
infant's dress! An infant! which wants nothing
to make it lovely and interesting! At first it
receives neither pleasure nor injury from the
beauty of its attire; for, in ornament, simply
considered, there is no evil: but presently
the child grows susceptible of injurious feelings. The new shoes, the fine hat, or frock,
is promised as a reward for good behaviour;
is admired by every good-natured friend to
whom it is shown; and no wonder if objects
thus recommended become deeply and per-
manently interesting. How lamentable, that
some of the first lessons conveyed to the mind
should be in direct opposition to the divine
mandate; not to be solicitous about what we
shall eat, or what we shall drink, or wherewithal we shall be clothed!

If to be *genteel* is the object, some of my
readers might be informed, that in decking
their children with finery, they depart from
the general practice of the rich and elegant:
children in such families are, with few exceptions, distinguished by the plainness of their

attire; and whatever taste for dress they in
future evince, it is a foible which seldom originates in the nursery. It is not till the period
at which education is said to be finished, and
young ladies are ' brought out,' to exhibit the
effect of theirs to the world, that much super-
fluity of ornament is permitted by mothers who
are really *genteel*.

It is an error very prevalent, but much
to be deplored, that the *nursery*, of all places,
should be destitute of neatness. Order, cleanliness, and regularity, have the happiest influence on the human mind, and contribute
more to keep the temper placid, and the head
clear, than many people are aware of. ' Let
every thing be done decently and in order,' is
a precept that should be extended from our
religious concerns to all the affairs of life ;
and where this invaluable principle is asso-
ciated with the habits of childhood, it may
reasonably be expected to pervade the subsequent conduct, and contribute largely to
individual and domestic happiness. Children
who are always accustomed to replace their

toys when done with; to make no unnecessary dirt or litter; to be punctual in their observance of time and place; will, even from the force of habit, practise the same regularity in more important concerns, on which the prosperity of future families may depend. It is to be regretted that males are so generally neglected in this respect; even where, with the females, it is strictly attended to. This negligence originates in the mistaken notion of its being out of a boy's department to be neat and observant. It is not likely that, with the utmost care, he should become too much so, if that care is judiciously exercised; and habits of regularity are as advantageous to him as to his sister. Beside which, the comfort accruing both to mistresses and servants, where the males of a family have been so instructed, none but mistresses and servants can duly appreciate. The only evil that could result to the young men themselves, would be in the event of their future connexion with females of opposite habits.

It would contribute much to the comfort of
families, without in the least interfering with
that of children, if some reasonable bounds
were set to the noise and clamour with which
people suffer themselves to be annoyed, because
they suppose it unavoidable. Children certainly might be accustomed to quiet at certain
times and in certain places: and those who
question the practicability of this, have only
to recollect what wonders have been done with
the brute species by the force of habit merely.
Are children less teachable than brutes?—A
gentleman once seeing a child much hurt by a
fall, expressed his surprise that he did not cry.
' I must not cry in the parlour,' said the child.
And what injury did he sustain by this prohi-
bition? Perhaps by the time he had reached
the nursery the pain had subsided, and he felt
no inclination to cry at all. Unless, however,
such prohibitions originate in rational motives,
motives which children will soon perceive to be
rational, little benefit will be derived from
them beyond present quiet. A family of eight
or nine children, who had been placed under

the most unreasonable restrictions, and rendered almost mutes by the father's caprice, evinced, some of them by their future conduct, that they had rather been the slaves of absurd self-will, than the subjects of paternal government. The frolic of infancy and the vivacity of youth are so natural and engaging, that those who attempt to suppress them, rarely succeed in forming a pleasing character. It is only excessive or ill-timed vivacity that a judicious parent wishes to control; but of times and seasons the parent must be the sole and unquestionable judge. A word, or a look, should be a sufficient signal, and instantly obeyed.

Parents should recollect, that what is most fascinating in their own eyes, and sounds that are music to their ears, may be extremely troublesome and oppressive to others. It was the remark of a sensible woman, that ' People think *their* children can do no harm :' the noise, the disturbance, even the diseases of *their* children, can be unpleasant to no one. This mistake renders the visits of those who

are accompanied by a rude and clamorous
child, very unwelcome and irksome. As it is
allowed to trample upon the chairs and sofas,
to displace, break, and destroy whatever it
pleases at home; those whom they visit cannot presume to defend their own furniture
from similar depredation, but at the peril of
offending the parent, or at least of doing violence to their own feelings. It is astonishing
how much even superior people often depart
from the rules of good-breeding in this particular. But children must be kept in subordination at home, or they will rarely produce to their parents either credit or comfort
abroad.

It is painful to observe, in many families,
how much the due order of things is reversed,
by obliging the elder children to give place to
the younger: when, if there is any weight in
the arguments for *early* discipline, the reverse
should be the case. This species of hardship
and persecution has the most injurious effect
on the temper of both, as it is not by acts of
oppression and injustice that the feelings of

benevolence and brotherly kindness can be
cherished, either in the oppressor or the oppressed. Those who practise this mode of
appeasing their younger children, should remember, that the surrender of a toy may be as
severely felt by a child, as if themselves were
compelled to relinquish something of real
value; and that the sense of wrong effectually
counteracts the disposition to kindness, which,
perhaps, they endeavour to instil. A voluntary surrender of personal gratification should
be early encouraged; selfishness, in every
possible form, should be repressed : but
coercion, though it may form habits, never
forms principles, the only security for their
permanence.

However diverting the mistakes of infancy
may be, yet surely the sooner they are rectified
the better. Parents, frequently not content
with letting their children remain in ignorance,
really promote and perpetuate it, by the absurd
impositions they practise upon them; equally
unconscious of the injury they are doing, and
of the ease and facility with which they might

be instructed. They might improve every
little occurrence, read lectures upon almost
every domestic process, and make every utensil
a diagram, with scarcely any interruption to
their own avocations: and if, instead of a la-
conic command, ' Do this,' or ' Do that,' they
were to explain the reason *why* this or that
should be done, they would at once impress it
upon the memory, and dispose the pupil to
obey, from the conviction that the method
prescribed was the only, or the best means by
which he could accomplish his purpose. To
accustom children to habits of observation, on
passing events and daily occurrences, would be
more beneficial than the abundance of tasks
and lessons, with which their tender memories
are frequently loaded. Memory, it is certain,
must be early and diligently exercised, or it
will never acquire facility and strength; but
its labours must bear some proportion to the
growth of the understanding, or its exertions
will be fatigue, and its stores lumber. A
mind early accustomed to act upon what it sees,
will acquire a degree of vigour, and a power
of discrimination, extremely serviceable in the

difficult and intricate circumstances to which
human life is exposed. As much as possible
to excite the mental capacity, parents should
discuss their affairs in the presence of their
children, who will seldom make an ill use of
their confidence, unless there has been some
radical error in the treatment they have received; and this certainly should be corrected
before the plan proposed can prudently be
adopted. Where, from habits of integrity and
proper feeling, a child may be relied upon, the
happy effects of family confidence will soon
appear: they will take an early interest in
family concerns, and endeavour to promote
the general welfare, with a degree of thought-
fulness and self-denial, if necessary, that cannot
be expected from those who are kept at a
distance, and treated with strangeness and
reserve. Frankness produces frankness, one of
the most pleasing qualities of the human heart;
and this, family secrets and family parties have
a continual tendency to repress: so that children who have been brought up under this
system, generally acquire an unamiable cast of
character through life. But the necessity for

reserve and mystery decreases, in proportion to uprightness of conduct and rectitude of inten- tion : where these exist, there is generally little to conceal; and where they do not, it is useless to prescribe rules for education. A prior work must be performed; the cure must be attempted at its source, in the renovation of the parents. But this is irrelevant to the present subject.

Should any question the prudence, or even the practicability of the confidence here re- commended, they are assured that it has been persevered in with success in numerous in- stances; and that children who have been accustomed to hear matters of private concern discussed in the parlour, from a very early age, have never been known to divulge them beyond its precincts. But to this system one exception must be made: those who indulge in habits of domestic altercation or detraction, should certainly choose opportunities in which their children are absent; and a restraint of this kind might prove as beneficial to them- selves, as the child found it, who was not permitted to cry in the parlour. Few, it is presumed, would desire their children to withdraw for the purpose; and in the interval the humour might be diverted, or subside.

If possible, my dear young friends, let your children be strangers to scenes of strife: they will soon learn to espouse some side, and participate in the unamiable feelings which such scenes produce. Remember that ' all the wars of feeling leave their trace:' and even if you regard their external appearance only, be solicitous to preserve the countenance, that faithful index of the mind, from the expressions of passion. Those who have been nurtured amid scenes of domestic peace and tranquillity, though Nature may not have been lavish of her gifts, generally wear such aspects, as are no invaluable passports into the world.

There are, probably, persons who may regard some of the above suggestions as fanciful, or impracticable: but nothing has been advised, that has not been practised with success in numerous instances; and those who are convinced of their importance, would be richly repaid by making the experiment; to accomplish which, nothing is necessary but resolution. When Frederick the Third of Prussia suggested a plan for the performance of some extraordinary military exercise, and his general objected that such a thing had never been done or thought of: he laconically replied, ' It *has* been thought of, and it *shall* be done:'—a spirit, this, which overcomes difficulties insurmountable to a feeble mind. That resolutions thus formed should be persisted in to any effect, it is necessary that both parents co-operate. If to keep children in subordination, and to give a right bias to their minds, entirely depends upon the mother, she should possess more strength of mind and address than falls to the lot of *young* females in general: and what objects for commiseration are those who, convinced of the vast, the vital importance of their charge, and sensible of their weakness if left entirely alone, are obstructed in their arduous efforts, by him who ought most anxiously to assist and support them! A house divided against itself, cannot stand. How needful then is it that

both parties should unite in the improvement
of their common property; since, eventually,
both must participate in the consequences of
the good and bad management to which it
has been exposed.

So much has been written upon the comparative advantages of public and private
education, that it would be superfluous to
protract the dispute: and persons in the middle
ranks of society have frequently no choice,
but are obliged to be guided by circumstances. Yet, if there is any weight in what
has been already advanced, it is obvious that
schools, which do not abound in the means
here recommended, cannot be preferred.
Day-schools, where any sufficiently respectable
are within reach, may afford the best substitute
for domestic instruction, and natural instructors,
who forego, or are compelled to resign, one
of the most rational and pleasing employments
in which the human mind can engage, that of
rearing up useful members of society, and
ultimately inhabitants for the heavenly world.

It is surprising how circumscribed are the
views of many who call themselves rational people, and love to be thought so. With common
foresight they might discern the foundation
laid for diseases, and frequently death, by the
mode of living adopted in those schools, the
proprietors of which are not sufficiently remu-
nerated for the comfortable support of the children committed to their care. This vital evil is
not so prevalent as formerly; yet, surely, too
strict an inquiry cannot be made, before the
health of children, and perhaps even of *their*
children, is hazarded. It is during the season
usually spent at school, that Nature requires
more nourishment than at any previous, or
subsequent period. Dainties are unnecessary
and injurious, either abroad or at home; but
as much as a healthy appetite demands of
good and wholesome food, is indispensable
both to body and mind: more than this, it
would be a false tenderness to allow; and it is
the part of discriminating judgment to discern
the exact point at which excess begins. That
the mind, if not injured, at least derives no

benefit from the custom already alluded to, of
overcharging the memory with what is not
understood, many can bear their testimony,
who now reflect upon such severe penances as
the sorrows of ancient times. Childhood is
the season for sprightliness and vivacity, as
well as for instruction; and whether a great
portion of it is not spent in such drudgery as
must injure both the spirits and health, may
be questioned by those who have witnessed
the laborious exercises with which children at
some schools are oppressed. At any rate, no
task can be productive of benefit, which is
exacted as a penance: none can love punishment; of course, when thus imposed, no child
can love his task. An antipathy to the sacred
Scriptures is often thus instilled: and what
more effectual method could be adopted for
the propagation of infidelity, than this mode
of chastising the frolics of youth, by giving
to be learned, as a punishment, a chapter in
the Bible!

It is however but justice to acknowledge,
that there are many schools, the conductors

of which have adopted, as much as is practicable in a public establishment, a system of domestic education; and thereby afford a pleasing substitute for *home*, to the children placed under their care. Such Instructors have a strong claim upon the gratitude of those parents who lay them under so great responsibility, and repose in them a confidence, great as is the value of the treasure deposited in their hands.

The unavoidable evils, however, which have attached even to the best schools, most of the male sex *must* encounter: and many circumstances conspire to render the number of females comparatively small, who receive the whole of their education under the parental roof. Happy few, who are thus situated! who are trained up where affection is regulated by prudence and skill! where no pains are inflicted, or penances required, but such as are dictated by the tenderest love, and fervent solicitude for their welfare! If such do not prove blessings to all within their sphere, where are we to look for amiable characters in this lower world?

But that all do not prove blessings, we are constrained to allow. Where this, unhappily, is the case, I would say, do not publish your children's failings. Should their conduct be very irregular, it will warrant some suspicion of your management; and, in any case, you had much better endeavour to correct what is amiss, than to depreciate them in the esteem of others, and thus weaken one of the motives to honourable conduct. The consciousness of being suspected, or despised, has the most injurious effect upon the mind; while the hope that we enjoy the good opinion of our friends contributes, powerfully, to render us deserving of it, and frequently deters from unworthy actions. We find, accordingly, that those who during childhood have been accustomed to perpetual chiding, and frequent and public marks of disapprobation, rarely attain to any dignity of character, perhaps not even to common respectability of conduct. It is lamentable to hear parents say of their children, ' I got such a one to speak to them, for they will not mind me.'—Indeed!—Then it is to be feared, that the precious opportunity has gone

by, in which habits of obedience might have
been formed; and that an occasional reproof
from a friend will not produce any permanent
benefit.

And now, my young friend, before I quit
this part of my subject, I shall solicit your
attention to one so intimately connected with
it, that I trust I need not apologize for its introduction.   It is the treatment of animals:
the importance of attending to which, from its
influence upon the happiness of your children,
has, perhaps, never occurred to you.   In doing
this, I feel less hesitation, from being sanction-
ed by such a name as that of *Erskine*, who,
to his honour as a man and a senator, impelled
as well by humane feelings towards suffering creatures, as a desire to promote the
interests of society, laid the subject before a
British Senate.   The respect due to so august
an assembly, induces us to draw a veil over
the result: but as the efforts of an immortal
Clarkson, and his coadjutors, in a cause of
still greater magnitude, finally triumphed over
avarice, prejudice, and inhumanity; the hope

is not yet extinguished, that the laws of our
country may extend their benign influence to
the lower orders of the creation; and while
mitigating their unnecessary sufferings, aim a
successful blow at vice and immorality:
though it is not to the credit of human
nature, that we are obliged to inlist our own
interests in the cause of any creature having
life or feeling, before its appeal can gain
access to our hearts.

That this subject should need apology with
the humane, especially those of the female sex,
is surprising; but in such cases it must be from
want of thought, rather than of feeling; and a
few words will suffice, perhaps, to recommend
it to their consideration. That those domestic
animals which we retain, either for our convenience or caprice, have a rightful claim
upon us for their maintenance and good
usage, is obvious upon a moment's reflection:
and what subject is there connected with the
comfort of any creature that can feel, upon
which we should think it too much to reflect
for a moment? Yet almost every house fur-

nishes a proof that few have given themselves
this trouble, in what Miss Porter so emphati-
cally styles, ' that ill-treated and traduced
creature, the cat.' To what severe suffering is
this animal exposed from famine, in houses
abounding with plenty, where its cravings
might be supplied by the least possible attention, and no expense at all! Like all others,
when in a natural state, it is competent to
supply its own necessities ; or if occasionally
otherwise, it is no affair of ours : but when
once domesticated, though still a beast of
prey, it can rarely maintain itself, and has a
claim upon those who have made it their
property to assist in its support.   But poor
Grimalkin is often dubbed thief for life, and
doomed to continual persecution and neglect,
because she has no alternative between famish-
ing with hunger and those nefarious practices
which are punished by the unfeeling cook
with many a kick upon her naked ribs : while
those who would not wantonly drown, burn,
or scourge a poor animal to death, feel perfectly at ease upon the subject ; forgetting
that theirs is but a negative kind of humanity.

They would not neglect the bird imprisoned in a cage; but where is the difference between an animal *in* or *out* of a cage, provided it cannot procure the means of subsistence?

Some people's feelings are wonderfully hurt if they see an animal in good condition, while so many of their own species are in want; as if there were no difference between giving a *bone* to a dog, and the *meat* to a beggar: the former can always be done with little trouble and *no* cost, but it is not always convenient to do the latter. Those who expend or waste upon favourite animals what would really supply the wants of a child, and who neglect a single human creature in order to do so, have doubtless to answer for a cruel misapplication of their benevolence. But it is a question, whether those in general who state this objection, are any more charitable in this way, for their want of feeling in that. There is one who feeds the young ravens when they cry; who satisfies the desire of every living thing; whose tender mercies are over *all* his works. How amiable those,

E

who in imitation of the divine example, practise *universal* benevolence, and take care of
the meanest creature they call their own!

As far as cruelty, cruelty of any kind, is
tolerated in a state, its pretensions to civili-
sation may be questioned, and its views must
be considered as proportionally contracted. It
is no remote conjecture then, that, in tearing
the limbs from the agonized body of a fly, the
little urchin is inflicting a wound, which, at
some future period, shall be felt by his country! And, in the same act, what a blow may
be aiming at those who witness the scene
without concern! An eventful moment shall it
appear to have been when this minute germ of
vice, though in the estimation of his *tender*
parents only like a grain of mustard seed, shall
have sprung up and produced the most noxious
fruit:—fruit which may poison their latter
days, and eventually bring their gray hairs
with sorrow to the grave. ' IT IS ONLY A
FLY.' Only a fly! It might as well be an
elephant; its effects upon the tortured and
the torturer are the same. The refined Athe-

nians adjudged a man to death for dashing a bird to the ground which had taken refuge in his bosom; regarding it as an indication of present bad feeling, and a presage of future bad conduct. We may not approve of punishing thus by anticipation; yet we must admit, that the suspicion was very probably correct. But we need not refer to ancient times: a variety of names, by which the pages of modern literature are embellished, have enlisted upon the same side, and endeavoured, though hitherto almost in vain, to instil the feelings of humanity to the brute creation into mankind. That this in so many instances is without effect, is not surprising; for, if it is difficult to remove prejudices and destroy evil habits, in cases that have a direct influence upon our happiness, those whose influence is indirect or remote, though equally certain, are little likely to be regarded. On such, people will scarcely give themselves the trouble to think. Should the time ever arrive when the cries and groans of the suffering and oppressed creation find their way to the heart of man, and duly ameliorate his conduct, what happy

days may not be anticipated! For who could
lift a weapon against his brother, who, equally
from principle and feeling, would not wantonly injure one of the lowest brutes? The
stag and the hare, those amiable and innocent
creatures, would still bleed to supply his table;
but they would cease to be tortured, to furnish
him sport. There would still be butchers,
but not huntsmen; fishermen, but not anglers:
the lords of the creation would no longer
appear in a situation so calculated to excite a
smile;—mighty warriors, whom, with a troop
of dogs and horses, one might imagine in
pursuit of some nightly depredator; some
noxious beast, who had been devouring our
flocks, or scouring our hamlets, in quest of
the sleeping infant! of whom, in short, one
might imagine any thing, rather than that
they were pursuing a poor little animal, that
one of their fair wives or daughters might
destroy with the pressure of her finger and
thumb! Rear not up a sportsman, my young
friend; but, by the rescue of a fly drowning
in a cup of water, or by a morsel afforded to
a domestic animal, lay the foundation of more

kindly feelings; feelings that may be productive of virtue and happiness when you are
sleeping in the dust.   This subject cannot
conclude better than with the followiug ex-
tract from the writings of Mr. Pope:

‘ Montaigne thinks it some reflection on
human nature itself, that few people take delight in seeing beasts caress or play together,
but almost every one is pleased to see them
lacerate and worry one another.   I am sorry
this temper is become almost a distinguishing
character of our own nation; from the observation which is made by foreigners of our
beloved pastimes, bear-baiting, cock-fighting,
and the like.   We should find it hard to vin-
dicate the destroying any thing that has life,
merely out of wantonness, yet in this principle our children are bred up: and one of
the first pleasures we allow them is the license
of inflicting pain upon poor animals.   Almost
as soon as we are sensible what life is ourselves, we make it our sport to take it from
other creatures.   I cannot but believe a very
good use might be made of the fancy which

children have for birds and insects.   Mr.
Locke takes notice of a mother who permitted them to her children, but rewarded or
punished them as they treated them well or
ill.   This was no other than entering them
betimes into a daily exercise of humanity, and
improving their diversion to a virtue.   I fancy,
too, some advantage might be taken of the
common notion, that it is ominous or un-
lucky to destroy some sorts of birds, as swal-
lows or martins.   This opinion might possibly
arise from the confidence these birds seem to
put in us by building under our roofs : so
that this is a kind of violation of the laws of
hospitality to murder them.   As for robin
red-breasts, in particular, it is not impro-
bable they owe their security to the old ballad
of ' The Children in the Wood.'   However it be, I don't know, I say, why this
prejudice, well improved, and carried as
far as it would go, might not be made
to conduce to the preservation of many
innocent creatures, which are now exposed
to all the wantonness of an ignorant barbarity.

' There are other animals that have the misfortune, for no manner of reason, to be treated as common enemies, wherever found. The conceit that a cat has nine lives, has cost, at least, nine lives in ten of the whole race of them. Scarce a boy in the streets but has, in this point, outdone Hercules himself, who was famous for killing a monster that had but three lives. Whether the unaccountable animosity against this useful domestic may be any cause of the general persecution of owls, (who are a sort of feathered cats); or whether it be only an unreasonable pique the moderns have taken to a serious countenance, I shall not determine; though I am inclined to believe the former. Yet, amidst all the misfortunes of these unfriended creatures, it is some happiness that we have not yet taken a fancy to eat them: for, should our country refine upon the French never so little, it is not to be conceived to what unheard-of torments owls, cats, &c. may be yet reserved. When we grow up to men we have another succession of sanguinary sports; in particular hunting. I dare not attack a diversion which has

such authority and custom to support it, but
must have leave to be of opinion, that the
agitation of that exercise, with the example
and number of the chasers, not a little contributes to resist those checks which compas-
sion would naturally suggest in behalf of the
animal pursued. Nor shall I say with Mon-
sieur Fleury, that this sport is a remain of the
Gothic barbarity; but I must animadvert
upon a certain custom, yet in use with us,
and barbarous enough to be derived from the
Goths, or even the Scythians; I mean that
savage compliment our huntsmen pass upon
ladies of quality, who are present at the
death of a stag, when they put the knife in
their hands to cut the throat of a helpless,
trembling, and weeping creature!

‘ But, if our sports are destructive, our gluttony is more so, and in a more inhuman
manner: lobsters roasted and fish fried alive!
pigs whipped to death! &c. are testimo-
nies of our outrageous luxury*. Those

* Fish of all kinds may be previously killed by
putting them, for a sufficient time, into cold *pump*

who (as Seneca expresses it) divide their lives betwixt an anxious conscience and a nauseated stomach, have a just reward for their gluttony in the diseases it brings with it: for human savages, like other wild beasts, find snares and poison in the provisions of life, and are allured by their appetite to their destruction. I know nothing more shocking, or horrid, than the prospect of one of their kitchens, covered with blood, and filled with the cries of the creatures, expiring in tortures. It gives one an image of a giant's den in romance, bestrewed with the scattered heads and mangled limbs of those who were slain by his cruelty.

water. This mode should be strictly enforced upon servants; for, independently of the shocking cruelty, there is no need yet more to brutalize the lower orders.

No. VI.

SICKNESS.

YOU perceive, by this time, my young friend, that the task you have undertaken is both multifarious and complicated, were no other cares or duties to demand your attention: but, alas! you may be called to act a most important part in scenes which will require an additional portion of prudence, self-command, care, and skill. Rare, indeed, will be your lot, if, after rearing a numerous family, your matronly qualifications have never been exercised in the sick chamber: then will you be deprived of lessons which are among the most salutary taught by adversity; lessons which, as they foster some of the best feelings of the heart, are eventually productive of happiness.

It is not the object of these pages, to attempt more upon the important subject of

sickness, than a few general hints: but, before
I proceed to these, I would observe, that it
is less difficult to prevent diseases than to
cure them. Air, exercise, and habitual placi-
dity of temper, have more influence in this
respect than (to judge by their conduct) many
people are aware of. Persons who would
shudder at the idea of incapacitating themselves for the duties of life by intoxication or
other vicious excesses, often, by a criminal
inattention to their health, approach nearer to
the guilt than they are willing to own, and
produce the same effects, only by a conduct a
little less discreditable. That Being who gave
us life and health, has a right to expect that
we use all suitable means to preserve them
from injury, in order that we may perform the
various tasks he has allotted us, with alacrity
and cheerfulness. But mortal poison is disregarded, if its effects are slow and scarcely
perceptible. Because no *immediate* pain re-
sults from the want of air and exercise, people
neglect them till neither air, nor exercise, nor
medicine, can avail. They *feel* that they cannot exist without food, but they do not feel
immediately that they cannot exist without

exercise and air, although equally necessary;
they therefore persist in neglecting them, till
life itself, perhaps dragged on through many a
miserable year, becomes a burden, and such a
burden as those only who have borne it can
describe. It cannot be denied, that heads of
families frequently find it extremely difficult to
select any portion of the day for this necessary
duty; but they find time to eat and sleep, and
to do a variety of things, which they deem indispensable to the welfare of their families:
would they rank daily exercise among the
number of their necessary duties, how much
longer might their families be blessed with
their protection and support, instead of being
left orphans, as, from this fatal negligence,
many are; or, at any rate, instead of inheriting
such constitutions from sickly parents, as must
render their own endeavours to preserve health
of no avail!

But, with every precaution, disease is not
always to be avoided; and from being unable
to prevent, we must study how to cure. Many
lives are sacrificed by the officious interference
of the ignorant, who, when it is too late, have

recourse to medical assistance; and because
the physician cannot perform miracles, deny
his skill. This not unfrequently is rendered
ineffectual, by the ignorance or prejudice of
the nurse, which has converted many a heal-
ing draught into mortal poison: or what is
equally disastrous in its consequences, administered death in a quack medicine. If some
of these are good in their kind, yet they are
always applied at great hazard, for want of
skill: this can only be expected in a regularly
educated medical man. It is from his watchful eye alone, observing the varying or complicated symptoms, that any salutary effect from
medicine can be rationally expected. If this
is the case, how ungrateful must they be,
who, when restored to life and health, grudge
the remuneration which such services demand!
Yet these are the people who frequently estimate the skill of the practitioner by his external appearance, and place no confidence in the
prescription, unless he attends in a carriage.
But neither is skill acquired, or a carriage
maintained easily: a handsome income must
warrant the latter, and years of laborious

study and application precede the former.
Who ought to compensate for these, but
those who reap the benefit of them? On the
other hand, a liberal education should be accompanied by a liberal mind. It is presumed
that none will afford just occasion of complaint, but those who have not the advantage
of either: especially that none will be so indis-
criminate in their charges, as not to distinguish between affluence and mediocrity: or
will so afflict the afflicted, as when they have
restored a healthy appetite, to deprive of the
means of gratifying it.

If any attention is to be paid to, or confidence
placed in, medical writers, who with one accord
assert the importance of regimen, we should
expect them to be very explicit upon this subject when they attend the sick, especially as
they are continually witnessing the fatal mistakes that are made respecting it: but, as they
are not invariably so, it behoves the nurse to
apply to them for information, and having
obtained it, implicitly to follow their direc-
tions. It may be very useful to make minutes

of the proceedings of a sick chamber, with
the occasional observations of physicians,
for future use; not as a substitute for medical help, but as a guide to the nurse in her
department.

Every woman of sense and observation will
soon discover the necessity of keeping a sick
chamber well ventilated and fumigated. Many
people imagine, that if a disorder is not in-
fectious this precaution is unnecessary; not
considering that a *healthy* person could not
continue in the same apartment long together,
especially with a fire night and day, without
rendering the atmosphere unwholesome; and
that the diseased are peculiarly susceptible of
bad air, which contributes greatly to retard
their recovery. When the weather will permit,
the doors and windows of a sick room should
be opened daily, for a few minutes, and a free
current admitted, provided it be not suffered
to blow upon the patient, who will also be
much refreshed, as well as his attendants, by
having a hot iron put into vinegar and carried
round the chamber; and if slips of lemon peel

are strewed upon the bed, it will have a
very agreeable effect.   That a change of linen
must be dangerous, is a prejudice now entertained by the vulgar only; cleanliness can do
harm in no case : if linen be well aired, it can
scarcely be changed too often; and by these
means, rooms, in which the sick have been
confined many months, have been kept as
sweet and fresh as any other apartment.

Experience has proved, that the notion of
keeping the delirious perfectly still, may be
carried too far, at any rate in the early stages
of delirium.   The mistake of a distempered
imagination may be rectified, and the patient
rendered quiet and tranquil, for a time, by judicious management.   Let him, for instance,
be reminded in a low and deliberate voice of
the hour of the day ; the day of the week ; the
room he is in; who were last in it ; where
they are now gone ; with any other simple
occurrence that may have taken place in his
presence.   In this way let any extravagant
notion be rectified in as few words as possible,
to bring his ideas into a rational train : and if

these means are repeated every time there is a
disposition to wander, they will generally have
a very favourable effect. If it is true, as has
been asserted, that deliriums have been aggra-
vated by the flowers, and large patterns of bed-
curtains, it is obvious that too much care cannot be taken to chastise the imagination, to
simplify the ideas, and prevent them from
running into confusion: but this will not be
accomplished by leaving the patient to himself,
and suffering him to follow the vagaries of
a distempered fancy, and thereby increase the
irritation. When, however, the cause is removed, the effects will cease. The first
devolves upon the physician, but the second
may be greatly mitigated by the management
of a judicious nurse.

Those who have never before duly estimated
the importance of keeping children in subordination, will no longer withhold their assent,
when the child dies because it *will not* take its
medicine!—*Will not!* Some parents can boast
of never having heard such a word in their
families; and of their children's owing much

of their recovery, under Providence, to their
habitual tranquillity.

But, my dear reader, let me remind you of
what youth is much disposed to forget,—that
you may be sick yourself. Now, if you are
beloved by all around you, which I hope is the
case, their affliction is little short of your own,
perhaps it is much greater: their united anxiety
and fatigue have a claim upon you even in your
helpless state, and you will not be so absorbed
in your own sufferings as to forget theirs, or
give unnecessary trouble, when you perceive
with what anxious countenances they prepare
your nutriment: if, after all their pains, it do
not suit your palate, or gratify your wishes,
remember the fault is not in them, but in your
distempered frame; that not only your own
sufferings may be tranquillized, but that you
may greatly mitigate theirs by a patient and
grateful carriage towards them. It is true, that
in the event of your being taken from them,
the remembrance of such conduct might inflict
an additional pang: but it will also be admitted, that there is joy in such grief.

No. VII.

VISITORS.

SUCH as are in the habit of observing what passes before them, with a view to their own improvement and direction in future exigencies, will accumulate a stock of experience, of which they are wholly destitute whose minds have not been accustomed to such exercises. It was observed, in treating upon education, that lectures might be read upon almost every domestic process, that every utensil might be converted into a diagram, and persons might adopt a similar mode of self-instruction ; a mode which need not be retarded by want of leisure; as the improvement of the mind in knowledge and experience, is a process that may not only go on amidst the most multifarious avocations, but which may actually be assisted by them. Those who are unaccustomed to mental industry would scarcely believe what rubbish

may be converted by it into use; even that
troublesome lumber, as some people esteem
it, the chat of old wives! To this the prudent young woman will be attentive when it
falls in her way; because, at the worst, she
may glean from it some piece of useful information in the art of housekeeping; some
scraps of homely knowledge, collected by
age and experience, which her own good
sense may turn to account: she will find that
old dowagers do not invariably talk nonsense
or scandal.

Nor, if she has any taste beyond the sphere
of domestic concerns, will she be inattentive
to the conversation of persons of the other
sex. Knowledge is desirable in all situations,
if it be not obtained by a sacrifice of that
time which their peculiar duties demand; and
subjects of literature especially afford resources, of which the mind cannot be deprived;
a fund of enjoyment alike valuable in prosperity and adversity. Some sensible people
have observed, that they like to hear every
man talk in his own line, upon subjects, there-

fore, which he well understands, and with
which others are but partially acquainted.
Much conversation, neither interesting nor
useful to a common observer, will, by the
more sagacious and intelligent, be carefully
gathered up, and kept in store for future
service. Those who search the streets for
pins, rusty nails, and bits of iron, which others
have cast away as refuse, are thereby obtaining a livelihood; perhaps occasionally finding a
treasure. And where the mind is disposed to
similar industry, selecting the valuable from
things which are every day and every hour
passing before it, what a treasure is amassed
in the course of years! What a legacy to
bequeath to posterity! There is a tolerably
fair proportion of eyes, ears, and common
sense, distributed among mankind, would they
only apply them to the purposes for which
they were bestowed. Young people must feel
that they have much to learn upon most
subjects; and a young housekeeper especially,
who is anxious to acquit herself well, and
conscious of some awkwardness for want of
practice, will avail herself of every hint by

which her management may be improved; she
will gather up even the fragments, that nothing
be lost.

In the middle classes of society many feel
themselves perplexed at first in the entertain-
ment of company; but it would be irrelevant to
the general intent of this work to give that
minute information which such require. Those
who are in the habit of frequenting genteel
tables will learn, by proper observation, how
to conduct their own, as to appearance and
arrangement; and the culinary detail may be
learned, as far as instruction can ever teach
without practice, from a book, entitled, ' A
new System of Domestic Cookery; founded
upon Principles of Economy, and adapted to
the use of private Families. By a Lady.'
This work, though, like all others of the kind,
it has its defects, is, on the whole, the best
that has appeared, and is held in deserved
esteem by many young housekeepers. There
certainly is no part of domestic management
which requires more skill and address, in
order to unite gentility with economy, than

the conduct of the table. Some persons suppose, that they cannot preserve an air of hospitality without profusion : but they are egregiously mistaken; for, with a little management, a table may be genteelly furnished, at an expense comparatively small, yet so as will give it a decided superiority over the lavish, and even clumsy feasts, provided by many hospitable and well-meaning people, who, not knowing a medium between profusion and meanness, would despise, perhaps, that respectable kind of frugality which is here recommended. It has been justly remarked, that those who would study economy must learn among the rich; or, at least, the genteel; where an observant eye will frequently obtain lessons, which may be advantageously applied to humbler circumstances.

There is one lesson, however, which persons must frame for themselves, and which is a most important one to young people when they enter life. It is the proportioning of their acquaintance to their finances. Hospitality is a virtue recommended in Scripture, both by

precept and example ; and friendship, that cordial of life, can be preserved only by showing
ourselves friendly ; but when the love of company, for its own sake, becomes the prevailing
passion, it is no longer hospitality, but dissipation.   People of fortune are obliged, in some
degree, to comply with the customs of their
own society, whether quite congenial to their
tastes or otherwise, and could not make any
material alteration, without the appearance of
eccentricity ; an appearance always to be avoided, unless enjoined by duty and reason ; and it
is the part of good sense to draw the line cor-
rectly between necessary and unnecessary
singularity.   But there are many, whose connexions are numerous and respectable, who
would be warranted by their circumstances to
make some decided regulations with regard to
company, at their first setting out in life.
Such conduct, however, requires some forti-
tude, and must be founded upon a conviction
of its necessity, or it will not be persevered in ;
for, in many cases, it is similar to the cutting off
of right hands, and the plucking out of right
eyes : it is enforced, however, by innumerable

fatal instances, within every one's observation.
Of these, a single anecdote, known to the
author, may be introduced as a specimen.

A young couple, having a very numerous
acquaintance, were, on their marriage, presented
by them with plate and other articles to a
considerable amount ; and they naturally
thought themselves very fortunate in the pos-
session of such numerous and kind friends ;
(kind friends undoubtedly they were). Impelled by feelings of gratitude the young people
endeavoured to make returns for the favours
they had received, by frequent entertainments : the consequence, though difficult to
avoid, was such as experience would have
anticipated ; the presents they had received
became, in process of time, the property of
their creditors, while some of those who had
presented them made remarks on the impru-
dence which themselves had contributed to
increase, each one thinking that, ' excepting
me, they ought to have kept little company : *I*
was only one, and could not possibly hurt
them !' If further persuasives need be added

F

to such instances as these, they might be furnished by keeping an account of expenditure,
as has been strongly recommended in another
place. Were this plan adopted, it would
require a greater proportion of hardihood
than most people possess, to persevere in any
course of superfluous expense, the amount of
which would continually force itself upon their
observation.

There are many friendships, as they are
called, commenced in the early part of life,
which experience proves to be not worth pre-
serving: to relinquish such on both sides,
would be wise; especially where the number
still retained is quite equal to the means and
opportunities: and few will disapprove of such
counsel, but those who have nothing to do
either with their time or their money. Persons
of this description will, in general, be unable
to account for many of the strange actions
of men of business, and women with families;
and must be placed in such situations themselves, before they will suspect that many
of their friendly calls have been, if not too

frequent, at least ill-timed and protracted :
from the inconvenience of which, those of their
friends, who cannot conscientiously suffer
themselves to be denied, are without defence.
There are some who instruct their servants
to say they are not at home; and assert it to
be no falsehood, because the meaning of it is
well understood. It is but a gentler phrase,
they contend, for saying that they are unable,
or unwilling, to be seen. This certainly is
not avoiding the appearance of evil, nor is
it setting a proper example before servants;
who, in *their* acceptation of the words, are
uttering a round and premeditated falsehood,
and who will learn, by these means, to dispense
with truth for their own convenience occasionally, as well as for their master's. But I beg
pardon for this digression.

Before I quit the subject of visitors, I may
solicit the attention of my reader to what
cannot be introduced with equal propriety,
elsewhere. A prudent woman, who is sensible how liable she is to errors and mistakes
herself, will be little disposed to investigate,

censure, or ridicule, the domestic conduct of
others.   To hear females, after returning from
a visit, ridiculing the entertainments of those
who, perhaps, had been doing their very best
to treat them with hospitality, is painful and
disgusting.   It is true that such frequently
pacify their consciences by exposing the blun-
ders of their friends *only* to their husbands,
mothers, sisters, or aunts; forgetting that, as
these stand in no such relation to the person
exposed, the injury done is the same as if the
communication had been made to any other
individual.   *Habits of observation* here, it is
to be lamented, are too prevalent among all
classes; and the propensity to ridicule, though
sometimes a prostitution of superior talent, is
the common resource of a vacant mind, unequal to self-improvement.   Its own mistakes
and errors lie undiscovered, while those of
others, especially of the trivial kind, are sought
for with avidity, and magnified into importance.   They furnish food, without which minds
of this description know not how to subsist;
and which, by its noxious qualities, eventually
indisposes them for more wholesome nutri-

ment. But if in any degree, my young friend, you are unequal to the duties of your station, it is more than probable that you may, in turn, become an object of ridicule yourself; and however unbecoming it may be in others to smile at your incompetence, the smile, with regard to yourself, may be justly incurred.

There is one object upon which ridicule seems likely to expend itself: and it is lamentable that even women of feeling do not always scruple to indulge themselves this way; while many, from the solitary title of a wife, without any other pretension, suppose themselves at liberty to treat with contempt and ridicule females, as much their superiors in character as in years, merely because they remain in a single state. This is a species of cruelty in which both sexes are apt to indulge; but it merits unqualified censure, and should call a blush into the cheek of every female who has ever been guilty of it. Perhaps, ladies, some of these traduced and persecuted beings have been only more delicate in their choice than

you have been; or circumstances may have
arisen in this mutable world to prevent their
entering a state which they were qualified
to adorn; circumstances which have thus deprived you of the benefit of many excellent
examples. It does not invariably happen that
persons remain single because they are not
worth having, or that others are married because they are: an example of here and there
a married lady might, perhaps, be found,
which would prove the contrary. Her husband, it is true, may be known in the gates;
he may bear the marks of her negligence
about him wherever he goes: her children
may rise up, not to call her blessed, but to
set her authority at defiance, and to spread
the contagion of an ill-governed family far
and wide. She may be employed, too, in
manufacturing girdles and other trappings;
not to sell to the merchant, but to decorate
herself in unbecoming finery, and to instil the
destructive passion for dress into her children.
It is not from being a wife merely, that real
respectability can arise.

A few words upon an error into which some
young persons fall in the choice of their associates, and the present subject shall conclude.
Many are so blind to their real interests, as
greatly to limit their society to persons of
their own age: among these, if they are careful in the selection, they may, doubtless, be
furnished with valuable examples; and, upon
the whole, they are generally the best calculated to pass away a social hour. But are
all old people uninteresting?   None would be
so, if in early life they had accustomed themselves to *habits of observation* and thought:
but many there are who *have* availed themselves of passing scenes, have accumulated a
rich stock of experience, and are solicitous
to diffuse it all around, that the young may
obtain gratis, what *they*, perhaps, have purchased at a dear price. Many of them have
not forgotten how to amuse, while they instruct, and are capable of tempering the
dignity of age by a cheerful vivacity.   But
it must be confessed, that characters of an
opposite description are sufficiently numerous,
to account, in some measure, for the distaste

of which we complain : and what objects for commiseration are those, who, when neglected and avoided by all, cannot retire into themselves and find resources there! Would you, my young friend, avoid so forlorn a condition? Perhaps you are now caressed and courted by all your acquaintance : but what would be your feelings, were the case reversed, and your society shunned and avoided? This *will* be the case, unless now you apply to the cultivation of your mind. Youth and beauty will be gone before you are well aware; time is rapidly bringing them to their climax; then they will be on the wane; and, if these are all you possess, what a dismal prospect presents itself!

Place yourself *now*, therefore, at the feet of those venerable characters from whom you may learn wisdom; and do not adopt the foolish notion, that those of modern times must, in all respects, be wiser than their ancestors: history does not warrant us to view human wisdom as *so* progressive. You would feel indignant, were your sagacity and

experience put upon a level with that of a
girl at school; as doubtless she would, to
be ranked with a child in the nursery. Why,
then, be reluctant to admit that the aged
possess all the advantages that time can give
in a much greater proportion?

It is truly interesting to contemplate youth
and age, when united by congenial minds,
enjoying the pleasures of rational friendship.
If youth may profit by the experience of such
a friend, age is amply recompensed for the
instruction it so willingly bestows, in the
sprightly vivacity which endeavours to cheer
its drooping spirits, or the kind attentions and
voluntary services performed to its feeble
frame.

No. VIII.

KEEPING AT HOME.

I MIGHT feel some hesitation in the introduction of this subject, if I had not a sanction
which none can well dispute, that of the
apostle Paul, who expressly commands that
the young women ' be keepers at home.'
Now, I have applied to the learned to ascertain
whether the words in the original, or by any
possible rendering, might be made to contra-
dict what they seem to enjoin, since this is no
unusual mode of dispensing with passages that
may not suit our taste or convenience : but, I
believe, in this instance I am tolerably safe,
and that nothing remains to be done, as we
cannot refute the command, but to conform our
habits to the genuine sense of it. It is obvious,
however, that it would be impracticable for
females to observe and profit by the experience and conduct of others, and to perform
many of the duties which devolve upon them

in society, if these words were to be understood in their widest meaning: they can only
be designed to correct that propensity to
gadding, that disinclination to the retired occupations of home, which too many have evinced
from the days of the apostle to the present
time. If the heart is abroad, the footsteps will
follow, under some pretence or other. Those
who cannot resist an invitation, who seize
every opportunity, or create opportunities
where none exist, to gratify this dangerous
passion, should have such a text of Scripture
set before them continually, in all its forcible
simplicity and unequivocal meaning, before
they venture upon a direct breach of the command. It is surprising, that many who profess
a deference for the Bible, should act in this,
and some similar instances, as if no such injunctions could be found in it.

A thoughtless creature must she be, and a
cipher in her family, who inquires *why* she
must keep at home. Those who are habitually absent from home, underrate their own
importance, for their presence ought to be as

essential there as that of a general at his post;
and it would be no breach of charity to presume, that something must be amiss in such
families. Where children are thus frequently
left, it is impossible to estimate the extent of
the evil. Will it be thought too much to
assert, that society at large is eventually affect-
ed by it? Surely not; when the danger of
contamination, and the incurable mischiefs of
early impressions, are duly considered. To
what purpose is the divine injunction, if hirelings are as competent to superintend a family,
to take charge of the bodies and minds of
children, as their parents? But the utility of
every duty inculcated in Scripture is so clear,
and the performance of it so consonant to
reason, that obedience and happiness are evidently inseparable.

What a melancholy catalogue would our
newspapers exhibit, if, beside the ravages of
the devouring flames, and the midnight mur-
derers, those made upon the human mind by
the habitual absence of mothers, were faithfully recorded! If such a register were kept,

it would doubtless appear, that too severe a
censure could not be passed upon those who
abandon such important duties, for places of
public amusement. Mothers whose eyes are
suffused in tears at the pathetic scenes of a
tragedy, may, perhaps at that moment, have
the scenes of a deeper tragedy preparing at
home, in which themselves, at some future
period, may be among the principal characters.
And is there not another description of persons
to which, with much tenderness, similar hints
may be addressed ?   Mothers, who, in attending the public services of religion many times
during the week, are obliged to neglect those
important duties which, as mothers, Providence
has committed to their hands: we allude to
those religious societies where week-day services are customary.   It is true that the usual
attendance at such times is seldom too large,
and that it may be deemed a kind of index to
the state of religion in those individual societies; but it is not in general from the nursery
that the thin ranks should be filled up. Many
there are, who, without neglecting any duty, or
with but little exertion and management, need

not forsake this assembling of themselves together, this free-will offering from the time which Providence has intrusted to their disposal, and let such feel themselves doubly bound. But the God whom we serve will have mercy rather than sacrifice: and surely from those mothers who leave large families to the care, or rather to the negligence of servants, while they attend those extra services, he may demand, ' Who hath required this at your hands, that *ye* should tread my courts ?' Far be the thought of discouraging any, even mothers, who, without neglecting duties at home, can thus secure an hour from secular employments for their spiritual benefit. ' Come in, thou blessed of the Lord ! why standest thou without ?' would we earnestly say to such. Come in, and strengthen the hands and comfort the heart of him who serves in the sanctuary. Come in, and enjoy the blessing which, both in season and out of season, is ready to descend. But to such only could we thus speak : others might more suitably be reminded of that command which says, ' Six days shalt thou labour and do all thy work.'

Innumerable painful instances might be
adduced, of evil resulting from the practice to
which we allude ; and, among many known to
the author, one may be mentioned of a well-
meaning, but mistaken woman, who, during
the infancy of her children, pursued this system to excess. When they were arrived at
maturity, she acknowledged, with agony, that
she had not one who did not scoff at religion!
But the immorality of their conduct rendered
this confession superfluous. A religious parent
with an *immoral* family! Surely, if vice pervades the whole of them, it is not unfair to
suppose that there has been some important
mistake or negligence in their education.
' While men slept, an enemy has crept in and
sown tares among the wheat.' It should also
be remembered that servants, as well as children, suffer from the frequent absence of her
whose duty it is to superintend them; acquiring habits of idleness and irregularity, which a
mistress will find it difficult to reprove, and
still more difficult to correct, while thus remiss
in her own department. When she quits the
post at which she is stationed, and in which

her own interest is so deep, it is not to be
wondered at if servants quit theirs, in which
they have no interest at all: nor is it likely
they should be skilful in their business, when
the watchful eye of the mistress is so often
removed. Where this neglect arises from the
love of dissipation and gayety, she can scarcely
be pitied when suffering from its inevitable
effects.

But we have not yet mentioned the husband, the poor husband! Where is he all
this time? The parable tells us of one who
had married a wife, and therefore could not
accept an invitation: but if she is more often
out than at home, he will be induced to accept
invitations that may eventually prove to her
disadvantage. The man who is not domestic in
his habits, will rarely be kind: but where are
the charms of the fire-side; where is that
which should give him a taste for its pleasures,
if the wife, its chief ornament, is absent? He
is an object of the greatest commiseration,
whose domestic feelings cannot be gratified by
the presence of her whom he has selected from

the rest of her sex to cheer his social hours; and she must not be surprised if his disappointment eventually recoil upon herself.

To a woman of proper feeling, no pleasures could be greater than those which the society, esteem, and affection of her husband, the improvement of her children, and the due order of her family, afford. But, lest I should be thought too rigid, or be suspected of attempting to consign the young to days of toil and drudgery, I will suggest some sources of relaxation, for which they need not be indebted to the caprices of their acquaintance, and which are excellent substitutes for that unprofitable round of visiting in which some people pass their lives. If these were added to the necessary and rational intercourse which all ought to maintain with their relations and *real* friends, life would be rendered, even to those who have large families and much to do, not quite so gloomy a thing as some are disposed to represent it. Who, of my young readers, will not give me audience upon the interesting subject of *recreation?* But, before the pre-

ceding hints are dismissed, permit me to suggest, that instead of applying them exclusively
to your acquaintance, as perhaps might easily
be done, you for once reverse the order of
politeness, and appropriate as many as possible to your own use; as we have, in general,
more encouragement to amend ourselves than
others.

No. IX.

RECREATION.

LEST what I may recommend upon this subject should appear chimerical or impracticable, I shall confine myself to the relation of facts, and record what has been done by some who were strongly disposed to recreation, and willing to enjoy as many of the pleasures of life as its duties would permit. It must be allowed, that few could do exactly the same whose circumstances and situation in life were not somewhat similar; yet such as could not adopt the whole, might have been inclined to select a part, and model it to their own convenience, could they have witnessed some happy seasons, which have left effects as salutary upon the characters of those who acted in them, as they have imprinted indelible traces upon their memories. But it is necessary that the reader should have contracted a taste for literature, in order fully

to appreciate the pleasures here recommended.
Literary occupation formed one of the principal sources of recreation in the cases referred
to, and was accompanied by a variety of
advantages, which might not have been per-
ceived by a superficial observer.   But how,
it is inquired, could a wife and a mother, so
occupied as we are told she must be, find
opportunity for reading?   Ah! where are the
husband and children now?   How she could,
remained, indeed, a difficult question for a
long season: but at last it occurred, that the
hours of breakfast and tea might be devoted
to this rational amusement, without encroaching upon more important avocations.— While
the children were in the nursery?—No.—
One of the parents read aloud, while the
little auditors were sitting, and actually quietly
eating their bread and butter in silence.   And
soon, very soon, did they begin to glean fragments of knowledge; soon were their tender
minds enlarged by ideas imperceptibly im-
bibed, which years of school discipline could
scarcely have instilled: while to the parents
many a pain was beguiled, many a corroding

care forgotten, as the interesting page was
explored. Soon, too, an additional advantage
was derived from this custom; the children
were so early habituated to occasional quiet-
ness, that it became easy to take them to a place
of worship: and thus again, a common reason
for leaving them to the care of servants was
avoided.

And, even if they had been disposed to
altercation, yet many, no doubt, of such disgraceful jars as disturb the meals of numerous families, reputed to live happily, would
have been prevented. If reading thus twice
a day, in the presence of a family, perhaps for
a period of twenty years, were not to produce
some salutary effects upon the heads and
hearts of children, still parents might con-
gratulate themselves upon obtaining, by this
means, one constant source of gratification,
amid the multifarious cares and concerns of
life. Anticipating similar cares for their offspring, they will be solicitous both to inspire
tastes, which may thus afford a lasting solace,
and to render, at least, one portion of their

lives, the days of childhood, serene and delightful; affording them every innocent enjoyment, and, as far as possible, such as, while
they amuse, cherish the best feelings, and
improve the character. To contribute to
these desirable ends, the aid of birth-day may
be called in. The young mind has not yet
attained the pleasures of retrospection; it pre-
fers something in prospect. Age and experience halt and look back; youth presses
forward, and is susceptible of feelings all its
own, in the anticipation of future enjoyment.
With such feelings, in general, the early birth-
day is greeted; and seasons of this kind may
be improved to the happiest purposes, as
well as made subservient to innocent pleasures. They are calculated to soften family
feuds, to silence petty bickerings, and to
excite a fraternal interest in the bosom of
every individual. In summer, such days may
be commemorated by a country excursion,
provisions taken, and the repast spread under
the shade of a tree: while halting, one, perhaps, sketches the surrounding scenery; another reads; thus uniting profit with pleasure;

and on their return a little repast may be
provided: the whole concluding with devout
acknowledgments to that Being, who has
given life and breath, and all things richly
to enjoy. In the winter a temporary cessation
from usual tasks; the whole family assembled,
as for an extraordinary occasion, and other
significant preparations, may announce a gala
day; and the evening spent in drawing, reading, music, or any amusement congenial to
the family taste, will long be remembered with
affection and pleasure. In families of any
size, these seasons occur too frequently to
allow of complaints for want of recreation;
the interval is short between one anniversary
and another; and if daily reading be added,
and evening walks, the time cannot pass away
very heavily. Persons thus occupied and
amused, need not be dependent upon their
neighbours for zest and interest; they have
complete enjoyment in the happy circle at
home. Nor is it to a few families only
that the materials for happiness are confined;
most are possessed of them in a greater or
a less degree, within the narrow compass of

their own walls; but, while the natural and
rational sources of pleasure are neglected, life
moulders away, and at the close of it numbers
look back and complain of their scanty portion of felicity. They had sought it where it was
not to be found, in artificial pleasures, and had
overlooked the satisfaction and delight arising
from the performance of duty, from the ex-
pansion of domestic affections, and from cul-
tivating the intellectual powers: unhappily
they attached the ideas of confinement and
drudgery to every thing that was to be felt or
done at home; and when the foolishness of
man has thus perverted his way, his heart
fretteth against the Lord. Happy they who
learn early to prefer the pleasures which God
has provided, and whose minds are prepared
by him to enjoy them.

No. X.

THE STEP-MOTHER.

I F the task is so important, the responsibility so great, which attaches to a mother, with what caution should a female undertake a charge, in which she has not the co-operation of natural affection! I would earnestly advise my reader, before she surrenders her affections to a widower and a father, first to ascertain whether it will be possible to bestow a due portion of them upon those objects, in whom, if he does not manifest the deepest interest, he affords an insufficient security for her individual happiness. Should he betray an indifference to their welfare, he gives reason to suspect the weakness of his attachment to her who was their mother: and in this case, my young friend, if self-love do not interpose with brighter anticipations, an inference unfavourable to your own future happiness must be the result.

G

Should you, on the contrary, be able to form a pleasing and rational expectation of what he *may* be by what he *has* been, and from what he still *is*, to those dear pledges of his earlier affection, I would again entreat you to make a solemn pause before you enter into so serious an engagemest. When such a one takes you, he not only places his own happiness at your disposal, but that of others, dear to him as the apple of his eye. And will you betray his confidence, when the power with which he has invested you bids defiance to his utmost vigilance? Shall the circumstance of becoming a mother yourself, which is calculated to enforce the tender lesson, shall this operate against them; and, insensible to the feelings and *equal* claims of those you are bound to foster and protect, will you transfer the whole of your affections to your own immediate offspring? If so, it is clear that you love them not for their father's sake, but for your own; and this would direct the most amiable propensities of the female heart into a selfish channel.

Without in the least derogating from the
superiority of the other sex, she must be a
very superficial observer who has not discovered, that they are deficient in that species
of minute discernment, of intuitive penetration,
which enables women to feel their way through
the difficulties of the world, and often suc-
cessfully to combat superior strength. From
this deficiency, men frequently become the
dupes of artifice and criminal design. The
woman who has gained complete ascendancy
over her husband's affections, in general requires nothing but address to possess a proportionate influence upon his conduct. Nor
let statesmen, or philosophers, or heroes, feel
indignant at the assertion. Solomon, the
wisest of men, was seduced into the grossest
absurdities and the deepest crimes; not by
his *wife*, but his *wives*, for whom he could not
feel the ardour of concentrated affection. It
cannot, then, be surprising, if men of inferior
order, (and who is not?) should be unduly
influenced by the individual upon whom they
have fixed the whole of their affection; should
be first blinded, if such be her unworthy

aim, and then led, as her passions or caprice may dictate. Accordingly, we have beheld, with agony, fathers, whose hearts have been alienated from their own children, the relics of a once beloved wife, by false representations and incessant complaints. Every childish foible has been artfully magnified into a crime; if not obvious necessaries, yet every indulgence represented as superfluous, and either withheld or reluctantly bestowed. The new family have been suffered to tyrannize over their elder brethren; and, by a strange perversion, *they* have been viewed as interlopers or encroachers. Ah! my young friend! if your heart, and, what is more, if your principles, cannot insure better conduct from *you*, give up the father and his children, and leave him and them to the mercy of hirelings, who, in case of flagrant misconduct, *may* be discovered, and *can* be exchanged.

But, if this expostulation should come too late to prevent the danger, let your own tender infant plead in behalf of those you are disposed to oppress or neglect. You are fascinated by its smile: *they* would smile upon you, too, if they dared, or if they discerned any thing in your deportment to encourage them. Once they *did* smile on *their* mother; but, alas! her eyes are closed in death; as, indeed, yours may be, you know not how soon, and the darling of your affection may, in its turn, have no maternal eye to sympathize either with its sorrows or its joys. But, if its smile prove ineffectual, let its tears prevail. Ah! its sobs you cannot bear, you hush its little sorrows at any price: *these* weep, too, but their tears are disregarded; their moans are magnified into crimes; yet, if they have any recollection of her they have lost, theirs are not trivial sorrows; their little hearts may be unable to distinguish the cause of their woes; they only recollect that they once were happy, and they feel that they are not happy now. Yet all this may be the case when no just cause of complaint may appear to the superficial observer, when no decided ill-usage may mark your conduct: on the contrary, it may assume the appearance of solicitude for their good, of zeal for their welfare; and for their good it may eventually prove to be, though far from your real design; the afflictions of their youth may be blessed by the orphan's Friend to the improvement of their characters, and may give them a decided advantage over your own family in future life.

But, while they suffer daily from your unkindness, or, at least, from your indifference, it is probable that they gradually lose ground in the affections of their father. Were he to examine his own heart, he would discover that his love is less fervent than formerly, less fervent than towards his new family; and he might, by a judicious investigation of circumstances, discover also the cause, and, in a degree, become proof against the encroaching evil: but whether or not he may discern the difference, his family will, ere long, make the discovery, and he might anticipate, with little hazard of mistake, jealousy, strife, and discord, as the natural consequence; thorns that will beset his future path, and be too deeply rooted for his utmost care and toil to eradicate. Judge, my young friend, whether all

this can terminate in the happiness of her
by whose misconduct it was produced, or
contribute, in any degree, to that of her offspring.

One important lesson she may learn, from
reflecting upon her own feelings and conduct.
In proportion to the difficulty she finds in
conducting herself well towards the children
of another, especially if any thing really unen-
gaging exists in their characters, she will be
solicitous to educate her own, that if, by her
death, they should fall into similar circumstances, they may, at least, afford no *just*
cause for prejudicing their father against them ;
and that their amiable dispositions, confirmed
and improved by her judicious management,
may give them one chance, at least, for in-
gratiating themselves with her who has become
their *mother*.

There is an ungenerous error, into which
a female is apt to fall who becomes a second
wife ; she views her predecessor, though moul-
dering in the dust, as her rival ! Probably she

still exists in the memory and affections of her husband; and, if she was a worthy character, this ought to be the case: should he be one also, it certainly *will*. To become the successor of one so deserving and so beloved, is no light undertaking: yet, as every female excellence was not concentrated in her, it is possible for a man to appreciate the virtues, and love the person of a living wife, while he retains the most sincere affection for the memory of the dead.

View her, then, no longer as a rival, but as a partner in his heart, and never suffer him, by your conduct, to make a comparison to your disadvantage.

I would earnestly recommend to you the study of human nature: you need not travel far in your researches; descend into your own heart, and there you will be furnished with lessons well adapted to your purpose. When you have acquired some skill in the science, you will discover that *sympathy* should be an essential ingredient in your friendly intercourse

with all; but especially with him whose bosom
friend you are; and to sympathize with him
in his tender recollections of a departed wife,
while it gratifies his feelings, will enhance your
own character, and confirm his affection to
yourself. But if her memory should be held
thus sacred, with equal tenderness should you
regard the dear pledges she has left; pledges
which Providence and their father's choice
have deposited in your hands: do by each no
less than you would wish to be performed to
your own memory and your own children,
should they ever be committed thus to the
mercy of another, and you will secure the
approbation of your husband, of your family,
of society, and, what is of far greater importance, of your own conscience, and of
God.

No. XI.

TO THE HUSBAND.

You have heard, my friend, of the multifarious and difficult duties required from her whom you have chosen for your partner in life. You discern, that hers is a station equally important with your own; and that whatever place you hold in the estimation of society, it depends greatly upon your wife, whether your children attain the same eminence. You perceive in how great a degree your domestic happiness, as well as your prosperity, is at her disposal. If you have made choice of one whom your judgment as well as your heart approves; one who wants nothing but experience, to render her all that is valuable in a wife; your own duties and obligations will appear in a forcible light. What does not a man owe to such a treasure? On the day when you solemnly committed your happiness to her, she afforded an indubitable

proof of the most unlimited confidence in
you, by surrendering her liberty into your
hands, and making you her undisputed lord.

Should you sustain a fair character in the
world, suffer not her who has the first claim
upon you, to know of your amiable qualities
only by report. A saint abroad, and its
opposite at home, is an offensive compound,
and it is well if, in process of time, some ill-
natured tell-tale do not divulge the truth to
society: indeed, it is seldom that real character can be kept a secret long, even with the
greatest precaution. But, if it could, how
impolitic is it for a man to render his *home*, of
all places in the world, uncomfortable, as is
frequently done upon the slightest occasions ;
and often in cases where the wife is not properly responsible, or where it is evident that
she has taken all possible care to promote his
comfort, though, from the negligence of others,
without success ! He should invariably conduct his own affairs with precision and exact-
ness, and preserve the greatest regularity in
those whom he employs, before his wife is

made answerable for the negligence and blun-
ders of servants, or she and they, and perhaps
a whole company, are embarrassed and rendered miserable, because some dish happens
not to be seasoned to his taste, or to appear in
time. A man of this cast has mistaken his
companion for his slave.

It is allowed, that every man should be
master of his own house, a prerogative which
he may preserve inviolate, without in the least
interfering with that of his wife; and, in
general, it will contribute more to his comfort
if she is left to the quiet direction of those
concerns which are more immediately within
her province: that woman should not have
been made a wife who is inadequate to such a
trust; and if adequate, happy is she whose lot
is cast with one capable of perceiving the discretion with which she fulfils it; who knows,
and approves, the judicious medium between
extravagance and parsimony, and who, of
course, does not counteract her prudent endeavours to preserve it. In vain does she watch
over her own department with scrupulous care,

if the husband does not co-operate with her in
the system of economy, and submit with
cheerfulness to its necessary privations. In
vain does she attend to the minutiæ of expenditure, and retrench, if needful, every indulgence of her own, if he is spending upon a
larger scale. In that case, while the wise
woman is building a house, it is the foolish
husband who pulleth it down with his hands.

To what sufferings, on the contrary, are
those women exposed, who are not allowed a
sufficiency to defray the expenses of their
establishment, and who never obtain even their
scanty allowance, but at the price of peace!
Men who act in this way, often defeat their own
intentions, and by constant opposition render
those wives lavish and improvident, who would
be quite the reverse, were they treated in a more
liberal manner. It would not be difficult to find
examples of this ungenerous system, and its
disgraceful effects; but they are not required.
Wherever it is adopted, it is utterly destructive
of connubial confidence, and often compels
women to shelter themselves under mean con-

trivances and low arts, equally injurious to
their husbands' happiness, as to their own
characters. From such men, indulgence is not
to be expected : he who supplies usual and
necessary expenses with so sparing a hand,
will rarely be attentive to the extra calls of
sickness, or endeavour to alleviate, by his
kindness, the sufferings of a constitution, perhaps, wearing out in his service. It was observed, upon the subject of cruelty to animals, that
many, because they would not drown, burn, or
scourge a poor animal to death, think themselves sufficiently humane, though they suffer
them to famish with hunger : and does not
the conduct of many husbands suggest a
similar idea ? They imagine, that if they provide carefully for the maintenance of their
families ; if their conduct is moral ; if they
neither beat, starve, nor imprison their wives ;
they are all that is requisite to constitute good
husbands, and they pass for such among the
crowd : but as their domestic virtues are
chiefly of the negative kind, the happiness of
her, whose lot it is to be united to such a one
for life, must be of the same description. Even

the large allowance, ' Have what you like,'
is insufficient to satisfy the feelings of many,
who would be more gratified by the presenta-
tion of a flower, accompanied with expressions
of tenderness, than by the most costly indul-
gences they could procure for themselves.   A
delicate mind, united, perhaps, to a delicate
constitution, has little relish for luxuries self-
acquired.

A prudent woman ought to be made acquainted with her husband's affairs ; she has an
indisputable claim upon his confidence ; with
him she must stand or fall : he should not,
therefore, conduct her blindfold to the edge
of a precipice, and plunge her, unsuspecting,
into the gulf below ; nor has he any right
to complain, if her expenditure is sometimes
too liberal for his circumstances ; she cannot be
expected to act with judgment, if the ground
upon which she goes is concealed from her.

To render the married life happy, there
must not only be confidence, but sympathy,
which is an essential ingredient in its felicity.

Pleasure or pain, of whatever kind or degree, is never communicated to another, but with the hope of obtaining the cordial smile, or the ready look of attention and interest: and those who, either from want of feeling, or of thought, withhold them, have made little progress in the study of human nature. But, whatever similarity of taste may subsist in a married pair, the difference of their pursuits and avocations is such, as to require considerable watchfulness in this particular. Happy is it, where affection and a just sense of politeness co-operate to render them attentive to each other, whenever interest is expressed, let the occasion be what it may: and engaging are those tempers which are ever ready to weep with those who weep, and rejoice with those who rejoice, even in cases where little emotion might have been excited by the event or the accident, but that which arose from this kindly feeling.

But, if similarity of views and feelings is ever important, ever indispensable, it is so in the education of children. It is probable, my

dear reader, that your avocations will not permit you to take a very active part in this most
momentous of all temporal concerns: but if
your assistance must be dispensed with, at
least be solicitous not to retard. In one hour,
in one moment, you may overthrow and render
abortive the labour of weeks or months, and
make your children set at defiance her authority, upon whose wisdom and prudent management may depend the future happiness of their
lives, and, perhaps, the peace and tranquillity
of your own declining years. Should your
situation and circumstances be such as to permit you to superintend their education, avail
yourself of the privilege, for you cannot have
an employment more useful, more delightful,
or eventually more productive. How many
are there, who spend a great proportion of
their time in training animals to contribute to
their sport, who, to the unspeakable advantage
both of their children and themselves, might
employ the same time, the same energy, and
perseverance, in training man! And to what
comparative perfection might he not be brought,
if transferred from the care of one parent to

another, he passed only through different
stages of instruction and discipline, dictated
by the tenderest affection, and the wisest solicitude for his future interests! Where this
cannot be the case, and one half of such inestimable advantages is unavoidably curtailed,
allow the mother full scope for her exertions,
nor throw any impediment in her way, already
too perplexing and difficult.

As communities and armies are composed
of individuals, it is obvious that each individual must act his part, or the operations of
the whole will be retarded; nay, that if every
individual were to suspend his assistance, the
whole could no longer act at all. This, which
is true upon the largest, is also true upon the
smallest scale; it might be brought down as low
as the parlour, or still lower, to the kitchen, if required. Survey some apartments, where a number of thoughtless individuals are assembled,
and where the hat of one, the gloves of another, the cane of a third, the knife of a fourth,
the brush of a fifth, the handkerchief of a
sixth, and so on in proportion to the size of

the family, are left to bestrew the floor, the chairs and the tables. ' 'Tis *only* my hat,' says one ; ' 'Tis *only* my cane,' says another, without considering that a house full of *onlys* constitutes some one in it a slave, if every one will not take his share of the burden ; and that by the simple process of each individual resuming and replacing his own property, confusion might be reduced to regularity, as by the touch of a magical wand, at least with as much expedition as evolutions are made at the word of command. You who imagine, that upon this larger scale your feats would astonish the world, practise first upon a small, and begin the manual exercise within the walls of your own castle, where hosts of the enemy might be put to flight without danger of a wound, and where your exploits would be rewarded by the smiles and thanks of her who presides in it ; smiles of complacency, instead of involuntary expressions of vexation and disgust. Perhaps, if some portion of that spirit of order, that love of regularity, which she displays, were transferred to the shop or the counting-house, it might both increase the comfort, and secure the permanence of the establishment. There are some men, at least, who might obtain useful lessons from the domestic management of their wives; and those who require no such assistance, but preserve, upon principle, the strictest order in their own department, should not object to an equal solicitude evinced by their wives in theirs.

It is in general from thoughtlessness, from want of a moment's reflection, a moment's care, that this distressing negligence proceeds: and from the same cause it is that persons, otherwise quick in discerning, do not perceive, that, if to perform their little offices, every one for himself, is a tax so burdensome, it must be inexpressibly more so to that unhappy individual upon whom, in case of his negligence, the whole must devolve. Nor ought she to be thought unreasonable, for wishing good order to be preserved in her humble sphere; for, if from the bee-hive or ants' nest, to the mighty empire, order and regularity are indispensable, why should the

poor housewife's domain be excepted, when
all below, and all above her, are allowed
the privilege? It has so favourable and
pleasing an effect upon the mind of a sensible
woman, when the males of her family contract
habits of decency and order, and evince a
respect to her feelings therein, that it might
be worth while, were this the only advantage,
to make the experiment; especially as the
effort required would be so small. There is
something, indeed, so agreeable in the character of a *gentleman*, that there are few
females to be found with whose taste it would
not accord. A slovenly ploughman may be
no inconsistent character: there may, too, be
slovenly lawyers, physicians, soldiers, and di-
vines; nay, for any thing I know, slovenly
dukes and lords; but a slovenly *gentleman*
can only be ranked with sphinxes, griffins,
unicorns, and mermaids.

Something has been advanced upon the
subject of keeping at home; and, to the
woman who has a just sense of duty, home
will be the spot where her happiness is con-

centrated, whether her husband is there or
not : but if, after all her exertions to render
it agreeable, he takes no delight in it, and by
his unnecessary absence proves that he under-
values her society, of how much deserved felicity is she not deprived! He, methinks, whose
prevailing passion is for going abroad, has
little right to object, nay, should make the
widest allowance, if his wife should manifest
the same disposition.   And if she should, the
fate of that family may be augured with little
danger of mistake.   Should she not, her situation is inferior to that of his servants, who,
if they have cause for discontent, change their
master, and meliorate their condition.   It is
only criminals that should be punished with
solitary confinement.

But if, unhappily, husbands and wives should
rarely meet at home, it is possible that they
may occasionally meet abroad ; and here it is
of more importance than many married people
are aware of, that each should render to the
other that kind of honour, which is due to
such a relationship.   Many, indeed, who are

by no means deficient in real affection and
mutual respect, fail to express either in their
general conduct, and appear as if at liberty
to treat with peculiar neglect, that individual
whom one has promised to honour, and the
other to cherish. A wife is tenderly alive
to the kind attentions of her husband, whether
at home or abroad: and neither can more
gracefully fulfil the marriage vow, than by
thus giving honour, open and cheerful honour,
to whom honour is due.

As every man is mathematician enough to
know that the whole is composed of parts, he
might, by the most simple process, ascertain
whether the character of a *good husband* is
justly his due. Pounds are composed of
pence, centuries of moments, this ponderous
globe of atoms ; and so, in the most important
relations of human life, trivial attentions,
nameless kindnesses, habitual tenderness, go
far to compose the sum of its happiness. The
great outlines of a picture may be correct,
but it is by a variety of minute and scarcely perceptible touches, that it is rendered

beautiful and complete. Refined, indeed, is
the enjoyment of those who know both how
to bestow and how to appreciate this exqui-
site finish.

No. XII.

CONCLUSION.

AND now, my dear reader, should I be so happy as to have obtained your hearty concurrence with the foregoing pages; yet, could I know of your closing the book without discovering it to be incomplete, we should not part mutually satisfied. Hitherto I have said little more than the wisdom of this world would suggest; and, though thus far I may have gained your cheerful attention, it is possible that now you may take alarm, and decline the perusal of a subject, in which you feel, perhaps, but little interest, or suppose that you feel enough without further anxiety. But let me crave, for a few moments longer, that attention with which you have hitherto favoured me, and nothing shall be advanced that will remind you of sects or parties; nothing but what is clearly authorized by the sacred Scriptures; nothing but a few simple

H

truths, to which, upon reflection, your own
reason, I doubt not, will assent.

The Scriptures plainly reveal that there is a
great and glorious Being, the creator and the
upholder of all things, the sovereign disposer
and Lord. And as to him we owe all we have
and all we are, he has a right to our best
services : these, to be acceptable, must spring
from the pure motive of filial love; for he
says, ' My son, give me thine *heart ;*' and we
are enjoined to set our affections on things
above, to seek *first* the kingdom of God and
his righteousness; and not to labour, as if it
were our only portion, for the meat which
perisheth, but for that which endureth unto
eternal life. The apostle Paul was so convinced of the necessity of this, that he counted
all things but dross that he might win Christ :
and wherefore, says the prophet Isaiah, do ye
spend your money for that which is not bread,
and labour for that which satisfieth not?
Also of the two sisters recorded in the gospel,
it was she who sat at the feet of Jesus, to be
instructed in heavenly things, and not the

one who was cumbered with much serving,
that obtained his approbation. Vain, indeed,
would be your utmost diligence; in vain
would you rise up early, sit up late, and
eat the bread of carefulness, without having
Him for your friend, who alone is able to
establish the work of your hands, to make
you rich, and to add no sorrow therewith ;
for, though your indefatigable industry should
heap up baskets full and barns full, yet, without a heart devoted to your God, there is
a curse upon you, both in basket and in store.
The curse of the Lord is said to be in the
house of the wicked; and this not only in the
dwellings of the profligate and the openly
profane, of those who cast off fear, and restrain prayer before him; but of those, who,
in the outward forms of religion, call upon
him with their lips, while their hearts are far
from him; and of whom it may be said, that
he is not in all their thoughts. Of such
worship he complains, and compares it to
bringing the lame, the halt, and the blind,
for a sacrifice. ' Take them now to thy
governor,' says the offended Majesty of Hea-

ven, ' and see if he will accept them at thy hands.' What blessings, on the contrary, may not be showered down upon that tabernacle, which, when it is first reared, is devoted to God! The Lord blessed the house of Obed-edom, when the ark had abode there only a few months. And the pious intention of David to build a house to the Lord God of Israel, was rewarded by a promise, that the Lord would build him a house, that he would preserve and bless his posterity if they continued to walk in the ways of their illustrious ancestors. Then think not your house furnished or complete till you have reared in it an altar to the Lord; till that worship is established in it which He graciously approves. Morning and evening assemble your family together to solicit His blessing, and say, ' Establish thou the work of our hands ; yea, the work of our hands establish thou it.' O! if the hearts of all who bend the knee at such seasons were ascending in devout aspirations, and not wandering, as the fool's eye, to the ends of the earth, what rich, what abundant blessings might be an-

ticipated! ' Where two or three are gathered
together in my name,' says our Saviour, ' there
am I in the midst of them.' There is He
waiting to be gracious, though with our bodily
eyes we cannot discern Him. The Apostle
James explains to us the reason why our
prayers avail so little. ' Ye ask and receive
not, because ye ask amiss.' The prayer of
the wicked, the supplication of those who
mock Him with a solemn sound upon a
thoughtless tongue, the petitions of such He
will not answer.

You perceive, then, my young friend, that
one thing is needful; that the substance, as
well as the appearance, of religion is necessary to your prosperity, even in this world,
and how much more so with regard to that
which is to come! Not that any are promised
exemption from those afflictions, which are
the common lot of mankind. Even if among
his true disciples, you are expressly warned
by our Lord, that in the world you shall have
tribulation; but it shall be administered with
a tender regard to your real welfare; and

that portion, both of prosperity and adversity,
shall be measured out to you, which shall
eventually promote your eternal interests.
What your heavenly Father gives, he will
accompany with a blessing; what he takes,
he will amply compensate to you by better
and more durable substance.

That you should be diligent in business
has been the object of the foregoing pages;
that you should be fervent in spirit serving the
Lord, is the design of those which follow :
and, for this purpose, let us see what improvement can be extracted from some of the common concerns and avocations of life; nor shall
I be accused, in so doing, of sinking beneath
the dignity of a sacred subject. Scriptures,
with illustrations drawn from humble employments, and the commonest processes, and
meanest implements, are selected to exem-
plify important truths. The Prophet Jere-
miah foretold a national destruction by the
type of a decayed girdle; and the absolute
dominion of God over all nations, by the
similitude of a potter's vessel; by good and

bad figs, the restoration from captivity; and
by bonds and yokes, the important revolu-
tions that were to take place in the world.
Ezekiel, too, by a tile and a pan, by a vine
branch and by sour grapes, predicted similar
events: and our Lord especially abounds in
similitudes of the most familiar nature. A
net, with fish of every kind, illustrates that
most solemn of all events, the final judgment.
Stewards, sowers, labourers, debtors, leaven
hid in meal, a new piece in an old garment,
lost sheep, pieces of silver, and even a grain of
mustard-seed, are severally employed by him,
and set an example which we need not be
afraid or ashamed to follow. Let us, then,
retrace the path we have trodden, and see
what further advantage it may yield.

And if economy in worldly matters is indispensable, of how much greater importance
must it be in your spiritual concerns! The
days of our years are threescore years and
ten. This, probably, will be all your portion
of time, and it may be of much shorter dura-
tion: even now, for any thing you can tell, the

Judge may be standing before the door. With
what parsimony, then, ought you to husband
the fleeting moments! Money lost or squandered *may* be regained; but time, precious
time, can never be recalled. It is a treasure
of inestimable value; a value, unlike that of
other treasures, enhanced by its insignificance;
for, compared with eternity, it is less than
a drop to the ocean, than an atom to the
universe; yet upon it your eternal weal or
woe depends. To have squandered your whole
substance upon the vainest frivolities, would
be wisdom, compared with that infatuation
which devotes every moment of life to objects
of which you must shortly take an everlasting
farewell. If pence accumulate and become
of value, listen to the clock, and note the
fleeting moments, how rapidly do they amount
to hours; hours to days, and days to months
and years! How swiftly do infancy, childhood, youth, and maturity, succeed to each
other, till that period arrives when all the
vain amusements of the world lose their at-
tractions, when its busy pursuits no longer
interest, and the grasshopper becomes a bur-

den! It is wise to make temporal provision
for such a period; but awful will be the
case of those, who, when flesh and heart
fail them, have no better stores, than of corn,
and wine, and oil: these cannot support
nature beyond the time appointed for its
continuance; neither can they be carried with
us into the unknown land to which we go.
Naked came we into the world, and naked
must we return: but true religion provides
all that is needful and suitable for the faint-
ing travellers; it supports and comforts them
in the dark valley, and leads them on till the
heavenly country opens beyond.

Again, if that style of dress is justly cen-
sured that assumes the appearance of a rank
to which we do not belong, may it not suggest a caution against the false appearances
which too many wear, who impose upon the
world by engaging manners, and put on the
look of sweetness or piety, while the internal
principle is wanting from which they should
proceed; that principle which alone gives
value to the character, or which can satisfy

conscience, when the good opinion of the
world is bestowed. In vain, my young friend,
do you make broad your phylacteries, and
enlarge the borders of your garments; if you
are not what you appear to be, you cannot
deceive the penetrating eye of Him who knows
your heart, and cannot, like your fellow mor-
tals, be misled by fair professions and the
outward form of religion. King David was
so desirous of sincerity of character, that,
in the language of humility, he appealed
to the King of kings, and said, ' Search
me, and try me, and see what evil there
is in me, and lead me in the way everlasting.'

You may be disposed sometimes to exact
too much from your neighbours, by borrowing of them what you should have taken
timely care to provide for yourself: remember, upon such occasions, the parable of
those foolish virgins, who, on the sudden
appearance of the bridegroom, said to their
companions, ' Give us of your oil.' Vain request! It must be by the reality of our own

religion that we stand in that awful and decisive day. The holiness of our husbands, our parents, our dearest connexions, though it might have proved extremely beneficial as an example, and have given authority to their precepts, will not avail us when the period arrives in which every one is to be rewarded according to the deeds done in the body. Isaac, Jacob, David, Hezekiah, had irreligious children, the holiness of whose ancestors could but aggravate their guilt; and the awful line of separation will finally be drawn between many a husband and wife, a parent and child.

If the wholesome maxim of doing every thing in its proper time, of applying every thing to its proper use, and of keeping every thing in its proper place, were extended to religion, how beneficial would be its influence! There is a time for every work and purpose under the sun: a time in which to withdraw from the business and amusements of the world, to commune with our own

hearts, and with Him who is acquainted with
all their most secret recesses, with Him who
will be found of those who diligently seek
him. There is a time — a day which he has
called peculiarly his own ; — then would this
day be set apart to his service, and not
devoted to the pursuits or the pleasures of
the world. Then, too, a portion of every
day would be consecrated to Him, whose
mercies are new every morning, and from
whom cometh every good and perfect gift.
If all things were applied to their proper use,
much that is expended upon a vain appearance, or hoarded in the miser's coffers, would
be diffused among the poor and needy, would
make the hearts of the widow and the orphan
to rejoice ; and much more would be devoted
to the nobler ends of instructing the ignorant,
and propagating the Gospel of our Saviour
in the world. If, too, the heart were kept
in its proper place, we should find it frequently in Heaven, where its treasure would
be ; from the contemplation of which it would
learn to estimate things according to their

intrinsic value, and cease to be captivated
by that which moths may corrupt, and thieves
break through to steal.

Those who have sufficient strength of mind
to dare to be singular, when worldly prudence requires it, would do well to raise
their courage to a higher pitch, and venture to be religious, even in the midst of
irreligious connexions. The Apostle Paul
exhorts the Corinthians to come out and be
separate. This does not prohibit all intercourse with the world; for then, as he ob-
serves, we must needs go out of it; but it
should certainly deter us from compliance
with its sinful customs, and restrict the choice
of our companions to the few who also dare
to be singular.

Have any a jealous sense of the services
and respect due to them from their domestics? By an easy transition may such be
reminded of the relation in which they stand
to their supreme Master and Lord. Should
they be blessed with faithful servants, giving

them due honour, promoting their interest,
and performing their services with willing
minds; this cheerful obedience may become
a pattern for their own conduct towards a
higher authority, and they may be stimu-
lated to greater faithfulness and exertion in
the service of their divine Master. Even the
remissness and ingratitude of our servants
may furnish us with a lesson; and while we
feel displeasure rising against them, we may
ask ourselves, if there is not One who is punctual to His engagements, be our duties ever
so remissly performed; whose mercies are
new every morning, and whose sun shineth
on the just and on the unjust : though finally
He will reward every one according to his
works? Happy are those, who, at the end
of their mortal career, can lie down in the
grave and say: ' I have accomplished, as
an hireling, my day,'—' I have finished the
work that was given me to do.'

But if from the relation of master and servant we may derive such instructive lessons,
how much more impressive may they be ren-

dered, by contemplating ourselves in the character of parents, whether we are providing for the present or future wants of our children ; whether instructing or correcting them, we may be reminded of the methods of our heavenly Father with respect to us ; who himself adopts this illustration, and says, that if we, being evil, know how to give good gifts to our children, much more will He answer the prayers of those who call upon Him for superior blessings. While we require implicit obedience to our disposal or commands, we are enforcing upon ourselves the duty and advantage of a meek submission and humble dependence upon the universal parent of mankind. Those who study their children's interest, by inuring them to plain food and clothing, may carry the same mode of reasoning a little higher, and be satisfied with that mediocrity of condition in which Providence may have placed them. Give me neither poverty nor riches, is a more comprehensive request, than the proud, the covetous, or the ambitious, are disposed to believe; for it comprises the sum of earthly felicity. But

there have been those who, leaving this petition far behind, have learned in whatsoever
state they were, therewith to be content : such,
like well-disciplined children, do not choose
this or that ; are not solicitous about what
they shall eat, or what they shall drink, or
wherewithal they shall be clothed : but they
thankfully receive the allotment of their
heavenly Father, who is too wise to err, and
too good willingly to afflict or grieve his
children.

Hints for the sick chamber occupy a few of
the former pages : a view of human nature in
that state of suffering debility, is calculated to
call forth every tender and sympathetic feeling ;
but here, as in most other cases, good may be
extracted from evil, and improvement may be
derived from scenes of distress. When the
whole head is sick, and the whole heart is
faint ; when wounds and bruises render the
body offensive or loathsome ; we are warranted
by Scripture to regard it as an emblem of a
diseased and irreligious soul : this is the
metaphor by which those are described who

live without God in the world. Such, in
whatever estimation they may be held for
wisdom and sanity of mind, are indeed suffering a delirium of the most destructive nature ;
they are harbouring a thousand extravagant
fancies, and practising a succession of the
grossest follies. The language of Scripture
describes them as forsaking the fountain of
living water, and hewing out to themselves
cisterns, broken cisterns, that can hold no
water. When urged by their own consciences,
or by others, to the performance of religious
duties, they fancy a lion in the way, and that
they shall be slain in the streets; they grope,
as in darkness, at noon day, and they call evil
good, and good evil. Perhaps while every
means is used which skill or affection can devise
for the recovery of the body, these more important symptoms are viewed with indifference,
or treated with neglect: these wounds are not
closed, nor bound up, nor mollified with oint-
ment ; yet there is balm in Gilead, there is a
Physician there ; and He, who is skilful in re-
moving this spiritual delirium, has left us every
direction that we need. Those unhappy pa-

tients might be reminded, who, and where,
and for what they are; reminded, too, what
time of the day it is — if in the morning of
life, they might be urged to insure its ultimate
prosperity, by devoting themselves to the
service of their Creator, now in the season of
youth, while the evil days come not, nor the
years draw nigh in which they shall say, they
have no pleasure in them. If life is in its
meridian, a hint might be given, that many as
bright a sun has gone down at noon. The
aged might be warned, that it is the eleventh
hour, and high time for them to awake out
of sleep; that now the time past must have
been sufficient to have wrought the will of the
Gentiles. And if such ideas have never occurred, or been suggested before, in the sick
chamber their importance is enhanced. When
the world is receding from our view, what but
real religion is likely to produce that meekness
and patience which compose even the bodily
frame? what is there upon which the mind
can rest, when, from pain and anguish, the
morning cry is, 'Would God it were even!'
and the evening, 'Would God it were morn-

ing!' What consolation, when flesh and heart fail, can be devised, if God be not the strength of the heart, and the portion for ever? In the sick chamber the severest measures are often prescribed, and the sharpest pains inflicted, to promote recovery; yet it is there, too, that, after all have proved ineffectual, the only means are withheld which could, in such hopeless circumstances, afford relief — withheld, from the cruel fear of exciting alarm! Thus many a one, totally unprepared for another world, is suffered to launch away, and to pass that gulf which will for ever prevent his return to afford those salutary warnings to his brethren, of which he had been deprived.

Habits of observation are recommended in our temporal concerns; but what ample field and inducement has the Christian to reflect and observe! Prosperity and adversity, whether sustained by himself or others, afford equal materials, and may alike be turned to good account. ' Whoso is wise, and will observe these things, even he shall see the loving kindness of the Lord.' He looks back,

and the design of many a mysterious providence is unfolded.

> Hopes, blighted by a Father's care,
> Perchance to save him from despair :
> And fears, whose giant armies fled,
> Dispell'd by Faith's courageous tread.

And thus, to him, tribulation worketh
patience; and patience, experience; and experience, hope. To him these words of the
Apostle are addressed: ' All things are yours,
whether life or death, or things present, or
things to come.'

Whatever may be our habits and propensities now, we all hope to arrive at that habita-
tion, where we shall *go no more out.* And, as
the church below is an emblem of that above,
we should do well, as far as we are able, to
preserve this part of the resemblance. When,
therefore, my dear reader, Providence or choice
has cast your lot in any particular society of
Christians, where the gospel is faithfully
preached, and those ordinances are administered which your judgment approves as the

institutions of Heaven: ' Into whatsoever house
ye enter, there abide, go not from house to
house;' be not seduced by itching ears, by
vain curiosity, or a fastidious spirit. If your
domestic concerns would suffer from your frequent absence, the religious society to which
you belong is injured in a proportionate degree
by similar conduct. No love for your spiritual teachers; no Christian fellowship among
brethren, which is the cement of every church,
could exist, if all were thus guilty: and yet all
have an equal right. It is those who are
planted in the house of the Lord, that flourish
in the courts of our God, while the most
vigorous growth will droop and decay in
repeated removal from one soil to another.
Nor is any one too insignificant to be useful; every pin of the tabernacle had its design,
and could not be removed without endanger-
ing the whole. Consider yourself as one part
of the church to which you belong; and be as
anxious to promote its interests, to preserve
order and regularity in all its members, yourself especially, as you are to maintain it in
your household. A woman is not permitted

to speak in the church, but she may render it as much service as many who do, by her constant attendance; by the example of her chaste conversation, coupled with fear; and by that meek and quiet spirit, which, in the sight of God, is of great price. Habits of constant and regular attendance have also the most beneficial effects upon the rising generation. Children who, in imitation of their parents, are accustomed to wander from place to place, will be in danger, as they can possess no particular attachment to any, of frequenting none at all: having never been taught to esteem their spiritual pastors very highly for their work's sake, it will not be strange, or uncommon, if in process of time they undervalue the work itself, and become indifferent about religion.

To your husband I have addressed a few words; that being with whom you must travel in company through all the intricate windings of this mortal life. Whether you rise to an eminence, and find yourselves exalted above many; or whether you descend into the vale,

or traverse the rugged and dangerous road,
you have sworn to travel together.   The laws
of God and man have united you in indisso-
luble bonds: but there is an enemy who will
one day, with relentless hand, cut them in
sunder.   You must part! ah! you must part!
And should you be the survivor, a severer
trial cannot befall you, than when the endear-
ed companion of so many interesting events,
the participator in every joy and every sorrow,
the desire of your eyes, the better half of yourself, is taken away with a stroke!   Where real
affection has existed, founded upon esteem, it
is a breach that is not soon or easily repaired.
Yet there are consolations even here.   That
divine promise has frequently been applied as
a cordial to the drooping spirits, ' Thy Maker
is thy husband; the Lord of Hosts is his name:'
and, ' Leave thy fatherless children, and let
thy widows trust in Me;' has been felt of
greater value, in such circumstances, than the
most ample provision.   But additional consolation may be derived from a retrospect of
your own conduct : when the remembrance of
past proofs of love, of endearments now for

ever ceased, would rend your heart; your
sorrows may be mitigated, if you are able to
reflect upon a life of consistent affection, of
faithful services, of tender attachment and
unceasing solicitude to promote his happiness :
and if, in the prospect of the parting scene, he
could adopt the language of Christian affection, and say,

‘ Whene'er it comes, may'st thou be by,
Support my sinking frame, and teach me how to die :
    Banish desponding Nature's gloom,
    Make me to hope a gentler doom,
    And fix me all on joys to come.
The ghastly form will have a pleasing air,
And all things smile while heaven and thou art there.’
                                        Mrs. Rowe.

FINIS.

J. MOYES, PRINTER,
Greville Street, Hatton Garden, London.

Printed in the United States
By Bookmasters